The Ever-Open Door

'Memories'

Compiled and Edited
by Ambrose Tinsley, OSB

First published 2006 by
Veritas Publications
7/8 Lower Abbey Street
Dublin 1
Ireland
Email publications@veritas.ie
Website www.veritas.ie

10 9 8 7 6 5 4 3 2 1

10-ISBN 1-85390-999-8
13-ISBN 978-185390-999-3

Extract from *Tuesdays with Morrie* © Mitch Albom, courtesy of Black Inc., New York, 1997. Extract from 'A Passionate and Gentle Voice' by Brendan Kennelly from *Familiar Strangers: New and Selected Poems, 1960–2004*, Bloodaxe Books, 2004, used with permission. Lyrics from 'You Raise Me Up' by Brendan Graham, courtesy of Brendan Graham and Peer Music Publishing Group, 2001.

Every effort has been made to contact the copyright holders of the material reproduced. However, several have been adapted from the original, and many Sr Eucharia made her own.

A catalogue record for this book is available from the British Library.

Cover illustration painted and contributed by Seán McDermott.

Designed and typeset by Paula Ryan
Printed in the Republic of Ireland by Betaprint, Dublin

Veritas books are printed on paper made from the wood pulp of managed forests. For every tree felled, at least one tree is planted, thereby renewing natural resources.

Contents

Preface

The first time I met Eucharia was in the early 1980s. She was visiting my monastery at Glenstal and by a providential accident I encountered her. I was in the right place at the right time. What we talked about I cannot now remember, but a seed was sown. It, therefore, was not long before I made my way to Corofin, of which she spoke, to find out what was actually happening there. That visit was to lead on to another one and then throughout the following years to many more. I was truly caught! Indeed, when I was siting in her presence I would often say, 'I came because I felt the need of an injection of "Eucharia"'. At that she sometimes smiled and sometimes chuckled; she enjoyed it.

One of the attractive qualities of Eucharia was her sense of fun, but so was her ability to cook and to prepare a meal. Quite frequently when I was with her, and considering the possibility of visiting some other people in the area before returning home, I would become aware that she was also scheming. Then she would perhaps trot off to get some extra bits and pieces, but would always end up in her kitchen and my own plans would no longer have a chance. I had to settle for what she so tastefully prepared!

Both of these qualities, the humour and the hospitality, are mentioned by a lot of people in their contributions to this book; so too was her ability to chat of things that were of interest to whoever came. That was no doubt why everybody liked her and, perhaps without expecting it discovered that they had been influenced by what she said and by the strength of her own personal convictions. Apropos of this, what is especially worth noting is that some of those who have contributed became her fans when they were only children or had been aware that their own Church was different to hers. However, everyone who came into her orbit found a God who never judged but could and did embrace them all.

It is quite commonplace today to speak about the need to build communities, but people can achieve this in a lot of different ways. Eucharia had hers and she was very sure of its importance. It was not to be a part of anybody else's plan, as Fr Nash, her local priest, discovered for himself. It was quite simply to become a 'neighbour', in the best sense of that word, and that is what she did. What is of course remarkable is that there is no evidence that her concern for others was perceived as being nosy or intrusive. On the contrary, it seems that people found themselves relaxed and comfortable in her presence and so comfortable with one another too. Then they were more ready to reach out and help whenever any of them was in need.

Eucharia was, as everybody knew, a Mercy Sister. Drawn by the desire to help the poor she joined that congregation in 1936 at the age of twenty-one. Initially she spent some time at Spanish Point and in Coláiste Muire, Ennis, where she is remembered still for classes in Domestic Science, and especially for the chat as cakes were being cooked. However, it was not too long before the social needs of Co. Clare attracted her, as other contributions to this volume testify. This led her to begin a number of distinct apostolates, until in 1981 she moved to Corofin and so commenced the last and, as she sometimes said, the happiest period of her life.

To many, this most caring Mercy Sister was a blessing, but that blessing was the overflow of her own personal life of prayer, which was not without pain. Alone with God she could become aware, not only of his love, but also of her own inadequacies. One of these was certainly connected with the fact that she had never been professionally trained to teach or to engage in social work, although it seems from all accounts that she did both extremely well. Then later, that same sense of not being qualified unsettled her when she reflected on how much so many people looked to her for guidance. Yet again she never seemed to have been anything but a memorable help. In fact, her lack of self-assurance seems to have contributed to her undoubted charm, while in her quiet prayer she found the healing and the strength she needed to become the person that she was.

Before concluding, I would like to speak about another pain which worried her throughout the last part of her life. It came from the awareness of the gap which seemed to grow as she responded to all those who welcomed her into their midst and separate her from her covenant-community (that of the Mercy Sisters), which at times did not appear to understand what she was really doing. Yes, she worried about that. However, it is interesting to read that Sisters who were closer to her actually saw that she personified 'all that is good in Mercy' and that she exemplified so much of what her founder, Catherine McAuley, most admired. No doubt, as she looks down on both her covenant-community and those which grew around her in so many places, she can see that, in the Spirit, all were always being drawn towards and into that 'eternal mystery' which so totally enfolds her now, and will forever more.

Ambrose Tinsley, OSB
Glenstal Abbey

Introduction

It is a happy occasion for me to endorse this collection of memories of Sr Eucharia Keane RSM, gathered and given by those who knew her, since her death in March 2005. In this simple and generous gesture they have added to the preservation of her memory.

Eucharia was one of our countless Sisters whose long and fruitful lives affected many people in small and big ways, touching them with God's goodness, love and hope. Occasionally, their impact seems to rise above the conscious water-level of quiet service and faithful commitment and Eucharia was certainly one who made such an impact. These memories lead us to give thanks and praise to God for her and to deepen our own faith that God works through each of us in many and varied ways.

I knew Eucharia for about thirty years and I fully accord with the testimonies given here of her deep life of prayer, her palpable love of God and her gift of drawing others to prayer, peace and trust in God's personal love for them. She seemed to move easily between the worlds of ordinary life and that of God's loving presence. To her they were one and the same. Her life was a seamless blend of both.

I also concur that she had a burning sense of pain wherever people suffered, whether it was from want, injustice or exclusion. This led her to use her gifts of imagination, determination and motivation to bring about services such as Clare Social Services, advocacy for travellers and supports for families, for young people or for depressed people. Her hospitality was legendary and was most often the ambience in which she showed and shared her deep love for God and for those around her.

Eucharia was a woman of integrity and sought to live a truly simple life without trappings or self-interest. Her desire to be a good neighbour indicated her preference for the local and immediate reality of people. She could respond in freedom and ease to whatever called to her at the moment. The constraints of organised religion and even of congregational life often frustrated her. Chapters, meetings, discussions seemed such a waste of time. Like Catherine McAuley she saw that if people needed help they needed it today and not next week. She needed to be free to respond and her final years in Corofin certainly gave her that in good measure.

Eucharia had a restless hunger for God that was never fully satisfied. She sought to assuage it by going to contemplative situations from time to time, but found herself caught up in supporting and consoling people once again, drawing her back into the lives of others as a woman of mercy and compassion. May the Lord she loved fulfil all her desires now and may she intercede for us as we continue on the journey.

We are indebted especially to the people of Corofin, who provided most of the memories, and to Fr Ambrose (Glenstal Abbey) and Sr Geraldine Collins for facilitating their publication.

Sr Helena O'Donoghue
Provincial Leader
Christmas 2005

Chronology

1915   **Born (11 December)**
Attended the Ursuline School in Thurles.

1936   **Entered the Mercy Convent in Ennis (St Xavier's) on 2 February**

1938   **Made First Profession as a Sister of Mercy on 15 October**
Taught in Coláiste Muire, Ennis.

1941   **Made Final Profession as a Sister of Mercy on 15 October**
Joined the community at Spanish Point;
Taught Domestic Science, Latin and Religion;
Attended the Tourmakeady College of Domestic Science Summer School for five years to train as a Domestic Science teacher (1943–1948).

1952   **Joined the community in St Xavier's Convent, Ennis**
Worked for three months (July–October) in the Orphanage in Ennis;
Bursar at St Xavier's, Ennis.

1961   **Taught in Coláiste Muire, Ennis**
Became involved with the Travelling Community.

1969   **Founding member of Clare Social Services**
Voluntary Social Worker in Ennis.

1972   **Moved to Limerick Social Services**
During this time she:
- worked with Sr Geraldine Fitzgerald, LCM;
- worked with Alexian Brothers;
- worked as a House Mother for outpatients of St Joseph's Psychiatric Hospital, Limerick.

1974   **Returned to Ennis Social Services (Clare Care) during which time she:**
- continued to visit families;
- organised a network of volunteers;
- started a Meals Centre;
- started a Thrift Shop;
- started an Old Folks' Comfort Fund.

During these years she periodically went to other places to pray or to serve the most deprived in society.

a) Venues for prayer and contemplation included:
   – Cistercian Monastery, Moone, Co. Kildare;
   – Holy Rosary Convent, Killashandra, Co. Cavan;
   – Adoration Sisters, Ferns.

b) Places where she worked with the deprived were:
   – Mercy Night Shelter, Crispin Street, London;
   – Centre for 'down and outs' in Leeds;
   – Dublin: caring for families living in Fatima Mansions;
   – Dublin: home for ex-prisoners in Ballyfermot.

1978 **Spent some months in the Mercy Community in Shannon**

1981 **Moved to Corofin**
Her time here, which lasted until 2003, was broken by two short periods, one to live as a hermit on Inis Oírr (1984–1985) and another to serve the people in John Paul Estate, Kilrush.

2003 **Retired with declining health to the new St Xavier's, Ennis**

2005 **Died: Holy Thursday, 24 March 2005**
Catherine McAuley House, Limerick.

The Family Background

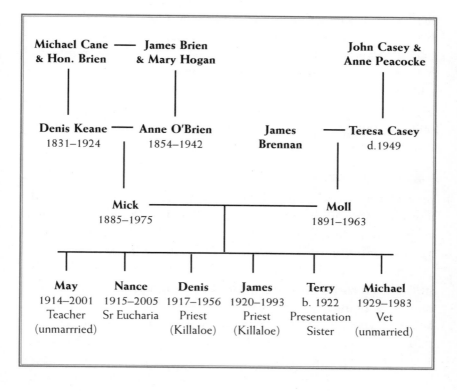

| Michael Cane & Hon. Brien | James Brien & Mary Hogan | | John Casey & Anne Peacocke |

Denis Keane — Anne O'Brien   James Brennan — Teresa Casey
1831–1924   1854–1942   d.1949

Mick ——————— Moll
1885–1975   1891–1963

May	Nance	Denis	James	Terry	Michael
1914–2001	1915–2005	1917–1956	1920–1993	b. 1922	1929–1983
Teacher	Sr Eucharia	Priest	Priest	Presentation	Vet
(unmarrried)		(Killaloe)	(Killaloe)	Sister	(unmarried)

My first cousin, Sr Eucharia, was always referred to within the extended Keane family and in the neighbourhood as Nance. Her 'Child of Mary' medal is inscribed 'N. Keane 8.6.33' (when she was seventeen). She was the second of six children of two teachers, Mick and Moll (née Mary Brennan), whose mother was a Casey. The Casey relations included craftsmen, a clerk of Templemore Church, two editors of the *Drogheda Independent*, a Dominican priest and a Peacocke great-grandmother, said to have been a relation of a Church of Ireland bishop.

Mick Keane lived to two months short of ninety. His father died a month past ninety-two and his mother Anne, after whom Nance was christened, died aged eighty-eight. Longevity was just one of Nance's inheritances. Her father, Mick, was reputed to have been a community leader in Longfordwood, Templemore, and his advice was sought on many parish and personal problems. In retirement, he recounted the foibles of country life with humour founded on a great feel, even empathy, for the vagaries of human nature.

Nance had both a similar counselling instinct and the same broad, wry outlook on social phenomena. The strength of her regrets for the deterioration in Irish social mores and in the world's concern for the underprivileged mirrored her father's strong opinions but were much more gently expressed, as in the manner of her mother's ease with the world as it was.

That the parents, with only Mick out earning most of the time, sent all their children for secondary and third-level education (albeit six people of good intellect) now seems to have been a fine achievement, even allowing for the input of seminaries and religious congregations for those who would be priests or nuns. Their dispersion in their formative years to boarding schools, however, loosened sibling bonds across the genders and to some extent within them too.

May, the eldest, was the one who kept in touch with all of them, with wonderful letters radiating love and by her gift as hostess. It was she who welcomed them to her Dublin home, to which her parents later retired. It was she who would then bring her parents to their children and to friends in Clare and Cork. And it was she who finally nursed each parent in succession until their passing. May's home also offered bed and board and loving care to the youngest of the family for his years of study and of early veterinary practice. All the while, keeping her Vice-Principal teaching post, she was the epitome of hospitality for relatives, friends and Dublin neighbours, and for those who travelled regularly to Drogheda to reciprocate the Casey visits. When May's health declined, including crucially her eyesight, it was Nance who brought a similar practicality to the rescue. Her Keane stubborn resolve wore down Keane stubborn resistance to change.

During this lengthy period, which was of great concern to all May's circle, Nance behaved as a Mercy social worker and enlisted help. When May eventually moved to a nursing home Nance consulted widely in the management of the house and of its contents. Then we saw her energetic and efficient, as she was in Corofin. She was at that time in her eighty-first year.

Nancy Murphy, my wife, who has researched and written on the early decades of the Mercy Congregation, recognised Eucharia as having gone back to the early Mercy charism of working among the people. It was clear to both of us that she herself lived as an ordinary person but with an extraordinary inner strength based on an all-pervasive faith which she shared with others in a firm and kindly way. She knew, however, she had lost me when, on one occasion, she was recommending some important book. Her wry smile comes to mind when my polemic, 'so, if the Holy Ghost guides the cardinals, how did they sometimes select such villains to be Popes?' elicited the reply, 'Maybe they weren't listening'!

Her deep spirituality seemed at times to cause a corresponding lack of interest in some temporal pre-occupations of ourselves.

But the warmth of her incisive words on public affairs, her pleasure in providing tasty meals, her ease in slipping into an educational mode on walks among the Burren rocks and flowers, all leave a host of pleasant memories – in tandem with an admiration for her multiple accomplishments in the varied strands of her own personal vocation.

Donal A. Murphy
Nenagh

Teacher and Carer

Eucharia came to Ennis in 1936 through the influence of Fr Dan Roughan. She had a great regard for the Ursulines in Thurles where she went to school and often quoted them, especially a Mother Mary whom she greatly admired. She didn't enter with them as they were enclosed at the time and Eucharia wished to work with the poor.

She was always conscious of not having been a past pupil of one of the local Mercy schools and often felt an 'outsider'. Some of the novices experienced her as 'aloof' and 'different' while others enjoyed her sense of humour and her firm conviction about issues, which she clearly articulated. 'She always had her own mind about things', they said. One sister remarked, 'We had great discussions, but I could never keep up with her!' Everyone agreed, however, that, no matter what the circumstances, she was always 'ladylike' and kind.

During her years in the Novitiate, Eucharia seemed to have had a very close relationship with her father, but the family seemed independent of each other so she didn't have a lot of contact with them. In fact, when the novices wrote home on a monthly basis, as was allowed at the time, Eucharia often didn't see the need to do so. However, she was very concerned for her parents following the tragic accident that resulted in the death of her brother Denis. She also kept close contact with her older sister, May, when she was on her own in Dublin and before she moved to Cork in order to be close to her sister, Terry, whom Eucharia also visited in later years.

Her deep commitment to Christ was evident from those early years. A companion remembers her saying, 'Wouldn't we have great regrets in heaven if we didn't do what the Lord laid out?' In her younger years she was very diligent about being faithful to the rule and to religious superiors, seeing them as manifesting God's own will for her. Her practical help of the poor, however, did not always meet with the approval of the Sisters. An example of this was when she wrapped a traveller's sick child in a shawl and brought him up to the fire in the convent. It is interesting to note that, from her early years in religious life, Eucharia's devotion to the Eucharist was just as evident as were her efforts for assisting the deprived.

Sr Teresa Meaney
Sr Frances Xavier Corry
Sr Paul Byrne

I remember Sr Eucharia with gratitude. My first meeting with her was in September 1939 when this beautiful, gentle Mercy Sister stepped into the classroom to teach Englisn and Latin to thirty first-year students. Class always began with a meaningful prayer and from that time one she was loved and respected by all the students. Later in the early 1980s Sr Eucharia came to reside in my native Corofin. She was warmly received by young and old alike. My mother died unexpectedly in January 1982 and I still remember the beautiful prayer session we had with Sr Eucharia and her wonderful support at that time of sadness.

At holiday time there was always an invitation to 'Emmaus', the house where Eucharia and Geraldine [Collins] lived, and I had the privilege of joining in the prayer sessions when I happened to be in Corofin. Sr Eucharia's hospitality knew no bounds. She became a real Corofin person and we all knew that she loved 'Sweet Corofin'.

Idir dhá láimh Chríost go raibh sí.

Sr Benedict Kenny
(Sister of Mercy)

Eucharia was well named. She radiated respect for the Eucharist. She radiated peace. She blossomed where she was planted and wherever she lived, and all who met her benefited from her gentle influence.

About 1954, Fr Mullaly, then curate in Miltown Malbay, said to me, 'You'll love Eucharia – she is coming to join the Spanish Point Convent staff'. I always hated the pre-conceived notion of having to like someone! But Fr Mullaly's words were prophetic and my pre-conception proved to be false.

Times were tough in the fifties and pupils at all levels were used to rigid discipline. Softness was discouraged. Along with the prevailing discipline of the day, the prevailing winds from the wild Atlantic buffeted us all. The youngsters, cycling the rough coast roads with their heavy timber boxes shielding the sacrosanct schoolbooks, suffered most of all. They accepted their lot and they expected no relief. What a haven of rest and nurture they must have sensed in Eucharia's class.

The numbers that entered religious life and the caring professions during those frigid and frugal fifties were astounding. Eucharia, smiling down on her many protégées, may now be able to throw light on this stoic idealism.

After our Spanish Point sojourn, forty years passed before I met Eucharia again. I knocked on the door of 'Emmaus' one Sunday evening. Eucharia answered the knock, recognised me and I indeed recognised her too. She was the same Eucharia transcending time, age and space, still ever giving of her spiritual peace and hope.

Suaimhneas siorraí dí.

Kathleen Ryder
Ballinrobe

I believe in your unconditional love
in every person –
Please give me the grace to respond.

Domestic Economy, St Joseph's Secondary School, Spanish Point: our year was beavering away on the sewing machines. My project was a blouse and I worked on it under the watchful guidance of Sr Eucharia, our teacher. I was not a natural at sewing, didn't particularly like it if the truth be told, but this gently spoken nun encouraged me every step of the way. Upon completion of the blouse I sat back, delighted with my work. I handed it to Eucharia with pride, hoping that my work would show the gratitude I felt for the help she had given me. The blouse was held aloft; I smiled from ear to ear – my shining moment! Eucharia smiled that heart-warming smile she had and congratulated me aloud, but then she bent down and whispered to me that she was very proud of all the hard work I had done but wondered where I intended to put my arms! I had managed to sew up the armholes of the blouse while attaching the sleeves. She helped me correct my error that day with patience and the minimum of fuss. While I did not go on to become a seamstress, or a Domestic Economy teacher, I learned a valuable lesson that will stay with me forever: life is never straightforward, but if you face it with a smile and encourage those around you on the way you will make their passage a little better for having done so.

Eucharia, you were a positive influence in my life. It is richer for having known you. Thank you!

Mary Macnamara
Corofin

What does it really mean to be a religious?
As I now see it,
it is to be a sign of Christ's love and compassion.

I was so saddened to hear of the death of Eucharia. I loved her. If you have read *Tuesdays with Morrie*, she was my 'Morrie'; she inspired me.

She taught me in Coláiste in the 1960s and everyone, even those who had no interest in sewing or cookery, looked forward to her class. She taught us so much more than Domestic Science (as it was then called) and she was one of the few teachers who treated us like adults. She gave me a love of cooking and homemaking that has stayed with me to this day. She always said that our class, 1967 Leaving Cert., was the best class she ever taught; we were so mature!

Eucharia was so far ahead of her time in terms of social service. She loved people and she had a special affinity with those in need of either physical or spiritual support. In the sixties she had our class writing Christmas cards to the patients in Our Lady's Psychiatric Hospital who had no one else to send them one. It is due to her, and to her interest in helping the less fortunate in our community, that Clare Social Services, now Clare Care, was set up. When I returned to live in Ennis in the early 1970s she collared me to help with a sewing group she had, making quilts out of old blankets for the elderly. Bit by bit she got me more involved in social services, and thirty years later I'm still involved.

I often visited her in Corofin and I know how difficult it was for her when she had to leave there. She never saw herself getting old and needing care and found it so hard to accept. She was so used to taking care of others. I visited her while she was in Ennis hospital but, regrettably, although I had intended getting in to Limerick to see her, I never made it.

I believe it is a measure of how close she was to God that he called her home on her feast day.

From *Tuesdays with Morrie*:

> *Maybe it was a grandparent, a teacher or a colleague. Someone older, patient and wise, who understood you when you were young and impassioned, and helped you to see the world as a more profound place, and gave you sound advice to guide your way through it.*

For me, it was Eucharia.
May she rest in peace.

Fionnuala Moran (Hensey)
Ennis

I do my thing and you do yours.
I am not in the world to live up to your expectations
and you are not in the world
to live up to mine.
You are you and I am I
and if, by chance, we find each other
it is beautiful.

Sr Eucharia taught in the school that I attended as a boarder in Ennis but I came to know her through her stopping to ask us 'lost souls' how we were doing. She seemed to sense our loneliness and isolation in this new world. Her person exuded a sense of inner calm and dignity and was reciprocated with a respect that extended far beyond what we as teenagers extended to any other adult. One felt a sense of being privileged when in her presence. She organised and facilitated an interactive, discussion group called 'LINKS' which dealt in an open and sympathetic way with many of the issues of interest to us at that time. This group had a spiritual dimension that made prayer and spirituality relevant to us in our daily lives. Sr Eucharia never forced an issue but let us reach our own conclusions through discussion and prayer. She was a gifted leader who practised far more than she preached.

What a lovely surprise it was to learn that she was living opposite me when I married and moved to Corofin many years later. It was a real pleasure to stop and talk with her on the road and come away feeling that the world was a better place after all.

She loved life and enjoyed nothing better than to have a chat with someone up the street. May she rest in peace with the God she loved.

Mary Healy
Corofin

Give a man a fish and you feed him for a day,
Teach him to fish and you feed him for life.

This old Chinese proverb sums up what Sr Eucharia did for me. She taught me Religion in my Leaving Cert. year of 1969. I can still visualise her in the classroom, her fresh complexion and gentle eyes. She spoke to us about life and about the 'facts of life'. She spoke about our femininity and our sexuality. She spoke to me in the silence of my heart. She made me aware of my own uniqueness. She instilled in me the principle that I deserve to be respected and, in turn, should respect others. This guidance has never failed me.

Sr Eucharia spoke to us one day about how to pray. She said, and rightly so, that we probably prayed to God-up-in-the-sky! She then explained that when we pray we should turn our thoughts inward to our souls. God dwells therein. Going home from school that evening I went into the church and prayed for the first time in this manner. In a matter of seconds my prayer-life had taken on a new meaning, and has changed for ever. Like the ancient proverb, she did not just say a prayer, she taught me how to pray. So many times down the years I meant to visit her but, regretfully, put it off too long. And now, by a series of coincidences, I am belatedly saying a big thanks to her for the direction she gave me on my life-long, spiritual journey.

Marie Burke (née Kennedy)
Loughrea

Men and women
have lost touch with the transcendent
in the world and in themselves.

Leaving her years of work in structured education, Sr Eucharia changed in 1969/1970 to a new and unstructured role in social care. In those times many did not understand why she would want to make such a move. That she was allowed to do so is a tribute to those whose agreement was forthcoming.

She became a full-time, unpaid worker in the newly established Clare Social Service Council, which could boast of only a small office and a secretary. It was uncharted territory and the officers and committee of the Council progressed on a steep learning curve. Given the opportunity for the first time, people began to come forward, seeking help with their personal problems and needs. Eucharia was well known in Ennis through her work in education and people were at ease in approaching her. She responded as best she could, improvising, befriending, supporting.

Meanwhile, the officers of Clare Social Service Council were intending to create structures for the care of the elderly in parishes throughout the county. Eucharia played her part in this while also working with the traveller community. By 1971 the work was progressing and uncovering needs and problems hitherto unacknowledged. It became apparent that there was an urgent need for assistance and for personnel with professional training. This led to a process that brought the first two Little Sisters of the Assumption to work in Clare Social Service Council.

A New Phase

Eucharia was now able to give more attention to some special areas of work:

- Meals at home for elderly people in Ennis – food being generously supplied by Mrs McKaigney, Queens Hotel.
- Visitation of troubled and lonely people in Ennis and environs.
- Clothing service, later developed into thrift shop.

After some time, and with the Little Sisters of the Assumption taking on their roles, Eucharia felt the need to go to work for a period in a more developed structure in order to enhance her helping skills. She moved to work in Limerick Social Service Centre, living in the Ladies' Hostel at the Good Shepherd Convent. She was assigned as assistant to John O'Brien, the Social Worker for St Mary's parish. In this work situation she gained valuable experience and she saw how the structures of the Social Service Centre had the facility to oversee and tie up the ends.

As time went on new avenues opened up:

- Friendship with Pam Stotter, whose work was linked with the Social Service Centre.
- Work with the Simon Community.
- A new pilot scheme to move psychiatric patients from the hospital to a halfway-house in the country on the city border. Eucharia took on the pioneering role of supervising and running the house.

Setting Out Again

Eucharia returned to Ennis in 1974 when the halfway-house project was secure. She set about taking up where she had left off, but she felt herself drawn into an issue that was exercising people's attention. There were homeless men in Ennis without shelter at night and there was no ready solution. Eucharia decided that she would go to work for a while in a large shelter in East London run by the Sisters of Mercy, Crispin Street. This she did and after some months she returned to Ennis in the knowledge that the needs of Clare's homeless people would require solutions on a different line to what she had seen in London.

Eucharia was a person who continued to pursue new challenges. Through Clare Social Services she got involved with others in:

- Organising the first thrift shop.
- Establishing a sewing group – ladies who prepared and re-made items of clothing. She had exceptional skill for this work. The members of the sewing group became her great friends.
- Setting up a meals-service at the community centre in Ennis, for people who came five days a week (later collected and transported). She managed this service for many years, later adding a chiropody service.
- Setting up with Pam Stotter the first community pre-school playgroup in Ennis.
- Developing a volunteer-staffed laundry service for house-bound people.
- Organising and supporting a corps of volunteer-helpers for community services.
- Playing a key role in the comfort-fund, designed to bring ease and little comforts into the lives of elderly people.

Pastures New
From the 1960s Eucharia had been involved in prayer groups. Later, her gifts in that area were utilised in providing spiritual nourishment for groups of people whose lives were hard-pressed.

There were days for these groups at the Clare Social Services' houses at Lahinch and Spanish Point. She also took part over the months of two summers in a special project in Kilfenora and Inchovea, living in a caravan, visiting people in their homes, with the whole project culminating in a parish gathering in the hall.

Eucharia continued with Clare Care until 1980. After she had moved to her new mission in Corofin, she returned over some time on one or two day stints per week to link up again with her former work.

Sister of Mercy

The foregoing is a brief sketch of Sr Eucharia's life and work through the seventies and into the eighties. These were years when she placed her great gifts at the service of people and their welfare. Through it all she was truly a Sister of Mercy. Reaching out and stretching herself in tune with her Mercy calling in each different situation! People in every segment of society recognised what she was striving for and they felt reassured in their own lives.

There was a pattern in her moving on, in her being able to move on, from one undertaking to a new one. That too was her gift. She trusted that, if the undertaking was worthwhile, there would be others to take it on.

Sr Eucharia – ever in pursuit of the good and of the God beyond.

Fr Brian Geoghegan
(former director of Limerick Social Service
and of Clare Care)

In the midst of all the violence,
abuse and appalling injustice,
God's Spirit as always is moving powerfully
among his people,
calling them to a more human and authentic way of life.

I worked with Sr Eucharia for a few years and my one regret was that she and the committee of Clare Social Service Council felt she needed a Social Science degree to continue with the organisation. I found her to be a gentle and kind lady who was genuinely concerned about people. I felt too that she had a special gift in dealing with young people – again I think they knew she was really interested in them. I know of one incident where young boys from Ennis went to Scotland potato picking and found themselves treated like slaves: locked up at night, little food and money. One of them contacted Eucharia, who was able to get money to them so that they could return home.

She had a fantastic sense of humour and we had many a laugh over the old battered mini car given to her for her many visits. It let her down so often!

Eucharia had a very deep religious faith and I suspect she had a special link with the 'man above', and at times would have ticked him off about some things that had occured. I have become a better person for having the priveilege of knowing Eucharia.

Nell Foster-Smith
Ennis

Sr Eucharia was responsible for bringing the Little Sisters of the Assumption to Ennis. I am sure this invitation was inspired by Sr Eucharia's awareness of the marginalised in Ennis, a great number of whom she had accompanied as individuals and in groups for many years. She was involved in the foundation of Clare Social Services in Ennis during the mid-sixties. Her vision was of a service that would cover the whole of Clare, what Clare Care is today. She recognised that the Little Sisters of the Assumption could make a contribution to that process of growth and to the care of the marginalised, particularly at the level of the family.

On the 8 October 1971, the feast of the Rosary, Sr Francis Collins, Sr Ann Kirrane, Sr Sheila Bunyan and myself moved into our new home in Ennis. My abiding memory is of the extraordinarily warm welcome and hospitality of Sr Eucharia. While this was her project, she immediately gave us ownership of it. Then, true to her nature, she moved on as the Spirit beckoned and, in the gentlest of ways, left us free to do our own thing. In so doing she gave witness to her greatness of heart and generosity of spirit.

Throughout the years I occasionally met Sr Eucharia and always felt I was meeting a genuine, mature, Christian woman who was totally dedicated to spreading the good news.

Sr Philomena O'Daly
(Little Sister of the Assumption)

In the early seventies, when I was working as a social worker in the parish of Rialto in Dublin, Sr Eucharia phoned me to offer to do some part-time, apostolic work. At the time she was helping to care for her father who was living on the south side of Dublin City and Eucharia had left her Co. Clare to be with him.

From the moment she arrived she was a beacon of light and life to all of us. She fitted in so well with all the activities going on in the parish centre.

With an old, second-hand sewing machine she was able to give sewing lessons to some of the mothers in the area. She also used her teaching skills in cookery classes and I well remember her making a Christmas pudding with some of the local women.

She had in her possession the original article on prayer written by Fr J. Borst, which was later made into a booklet. It was my first real introduction to contemplative prayer and for that I will always be grateful.

To work alongside Eucharia was a spiritual experience. She had great empathy for young parents who were struggling and she had the ability to set up practical classes to help them, especially classes for mothers caring for their children. I remember on one occasion we were both sitting in the car, looking at a block of flats and discussing how best to reach and help those people. Eucharia looked at me and said, 'Claude, we are not going to redeem these people because they have already been redeemed – by Christ'.

Sr Claude McDonald
(Little Sister of the Assumption)

Lord, I understand nothing.
I have no gifts.
I am nothing of myself
but I know that you
at times use my nothingness to help people.
May your will triumph in me and your love consume me.

Eucharia was in Coláiste in 1967 when I became involved in working for the travellers. I became a member of the committee. Eucharia knew the people and introduced me to the work. She herself was not one for coming to meetings but she was always contactable. The committee started by fund-raising for green canvas for shelters, as the travellers lived in tents at the side of the road. It then established a settlement group which strove to provide accommodation for the travellers. This was followed by efforts to provide education for the children and later to provide workshops for training for employment.

Eucharia eased me into working with the travellers by doing it herself, and she was very encouraging. When children were being prepared for Confirmation, Eucharia left me to fit out our six or seven young lads. So I had to go shopping and try to please everybody on a small budget. She was always hopeful and knew that things would work out all right. And it did; the boys and girls looked very well in the photograph with Bishop Harty.

I remember one Christmas Day in the 1970s when there was terrible flooding around Ennis. We were giving out hampers on Lee's Road. Traffic was being diverted from the main road through Lee's Road and a farmer who was rushing for twelve o' clock mass, frustrated by the delay caused by the traffic congestion, spoke in very strong language. Of this, Eucharia commented, 'I don't know how that man is going to recognise the Lord in a piece of bread if he doesn't recognise him in the people out here on the road'.

Eucharia was a woman of great faith and she wouldn't want anyone drawing attention to her work. Her strong faith in God was very obvious. She had the Lord uppermost in her mind every day and all the people she met were part of God's family. She always had a great understanding of the travellers and did great work for them.

This is a summary of a conversation with Pat Galvin
who has been working and caring for the Travelling Community
in Co. Clare for over thirty years.

Memories from the Travelling Community

Eucharia was a very friendly and nice person. She was a person you could talk to and she was very helpful. She knew the travellers before most in the community and she helped us with our needs. She would give us food, clothes, pants or a pair of shoes.

As young lads, when we'd be coming home, we'd call to the convent for a bit of dinner and we would be praying that Eucharia would be there. She was so kind; she'd give us a real dinner and would always have a bit of dessert. She was very kind, a great woman to listen and someone you'd be very relaxed talking to. We'd call more often because she was there and she'd love to see us coming.

Michael McDonagh

I used to meet Sister Eucharia in Coláiste and she was very good to the travelling people.

Mrs McCarthy

Eucharia knew the travellers when they lived in tents on the side of Lee's Road. At the time we brought home babies to cold tents which were often wet too. It was very hard to wash and dry their clothes. A lot of babies died at the time. At times, we even had to put out our fires and move on to another place. I remember when my husband had a horse-drawn caravan. He once had to dig the ground around the wheels and lift the caravan off the road. We had to go in the dark of winter and look for another gap in the road and we often had to dig the snow away.

Eucharia knew we had no way of cooking and would come to Lee's Road with a big tank of milk or hot soup and give it to everyone. At Christmas, she knew that we had no way of cooking turkey so she would come with a cooked turkey and dinner and with hampers of food and toys for the children.

I remember one other time: I was waiting to go to hospital to deliver a baby. I was in a tent; we had no caravan at the time. She brought me down grand things, nightdresses and stuff for the baby. She came to visit me in hospital and came again after I was back home, bringing toys for the children.

Eucharia helped get the children ready for Holy Communion. She took them and prepared them in the convent. She got them white dresses and brought us all for a big breakfast.

She started a mother's club where we learnt how to cook and make flowers. When we got the *tigíns*, we got stuff to make curtains for the house and Eucharia helped us. She was always kind to the travellers.

Mrs McDonagh

I am no specialist in the art of prayer.
Many listening to me
have a deeper relationship with the Lord than I have.
All I am attempting to do is to share some thoughts
that I have prayed over
and shared with the Lord.

You ask me what I remember about Eucharia:

- Her openness to difference and her respect for all.
- Her concern for the vulnerable from the stance of her own vulnerability.
- Her impatience with anything which militated against freedom or creativity.
- Her appreciation of the natural world and the beauty of God's creation, especially the Burren.
- Her friendship with me and with many others.
- Her sense of humour.
- Her warmth for the people among whom she lived and worked.
- Her affinity for scripture and the prayer of the Church as the source of her spirituality.
- Her honesty in admitting to things she found difficult to accept.
- Her welcome to all who visited her.

The message of her life is that God's love holds on to us no matter what happens and however far we may wander. God's welcome is eternal for God's love endures forever. I pray that I, in my own way, may follow in her footsteps.

Pam Stotter
Skibbereen

Words are inadequate to express our experience of people whom we love and who leave an indelible mark on how we think and live.

Such a person for me was Eucharia Keane. She has been a part of my life for nearly forty years. I had the privilege of sharing her love and of sharing the deep, personal thoughts and dreams of her beautiful soul on a variety of topics. It is rare to meet a real 'soul mate', someone who says what she really means and leaves you feeling better, stretched in your thinking and looking forward to the next conversation. In my life I have met only two such people. Eucharia was one of them and, though she is now enjoying the peace she so yearned for and deserved, her presence and influence are very close to me. She inspired me to think and to act beyond the boundaries of convention and orthodoxy within religious life and society. The result of long reflection overflowed into our relationships with the people whose lives, faith, joy, trials, tribulations and hopes we shared. There was a quiet transcendence of standard mores and sometimes a disregard for the tardiness of the religious, political and social structures within which we ministered. Eucharia lived for the person/people who felt or who were on the margins of life.

I first met Eucharia Keane in the early 1970s when she was on the staff of Limerick Social Centre. We lived and worked in years of rapid and constant societal change, in structures of all kinds, not least in those of religious life. The theological, sociological and liturgical changes emphasised by the Second Vatican Council were fresh, exciting and creating much enthusiasm in relation to bridging the gap between Religious and the people among whom we worked. However, these changes were not fast enough for Eucharia because she saw people suffering and as long as people suffered Eucharia would try to bring about a change in their circumstances. One of her outstanding gifts was her ability to interact with all age groups. Somehow, people got sustenance from her love, compassion and integrity and from her non-judgemental attitude. She shared from the well of her own deep belief in a loving, forgiving, all-knowing God.

Working close with Eucharia was very 'reality-based'. Her 'loving' could be demanding at times. When faced with preparing for 'Sunday Retreat Days' for up to seventy people or for catering for sixty to seventy constantly hungry youngsters, Eucharia could be very human. I can still see the dismayed face of a volunteer who, having worked hard to prepare dinner for seventy people, was admonished for not 'drying the chips' properly!

Another memorable moment was when we were preparing Catherine McAuley House in Limerick for opening. We were working late and, tired and weary, we decided to stay the night there. Sleeping facilities were extremely primitive. We opened covers which had 'Clare Social Services Council' imprinted on them to use as sheets. Just as we were about to go to sleep Eucharia said to me, 'we are not only working for Clare Social Services but now we are sleeping under its banner', pointing to the name tag.

Another very special time was when the late Fr Paddy Vaughan went on holidays and we were spending that time visiting in the North Clare area of Kilfenora, Inchovea, Carron, Liscannor and Blackhead with a view to having a mass in the parish hall, the first outside a church for many people. When he returned he was amazed to see how much altar wine had been used. People had been given Holy Communion under both species, something not allowed in the diocese at that time, although we did not know this.

During those summers we lived in an old-style caravan, parked in the square in Kilfenora. This particular mission took on a life of its own and finished with a service of reconciliation and with mass. We would set out each day and visit people in the isolated parts of North Clare. People also came to visit us, to share what was happening in their lives, to pray with us and so often to inquire if we had all we needed. It was during the many times of interpersonal sharing and planning that I got to know the real person of Eucharia, the woman who loved and worried about her family and their needs, the woman who enjoyed a glass of port or sherry, the great cook who believed in eating well, the one who never worried if someone might call because there was always plenty in the pot, the woman who knew the dryness of depression as well as the joy of light, the woman close to all aspects of nature, who cared for the earth long before it became fashionable to do so, the woman who enjoyed reading a well-written book, fact or fiction. She introduced me to Meister Eckhart and when I became familiar with his writings I realised how Eucharia had internalised his believe in transformation and how she practised being totally present to everyone.

Eucharia, though very active and never having enough time, was first and foremost a Contemplative, urging reflection on God's love for us so as to be able to share it with others. This was her underlying reason for everything she did. She drew strength from the Eucharist and I was not surprised that God took her to himself on the Feast of the Eucharist. She deserved nothing less.

I am a better, more fulfilled person for having known Eucharia.

Ar dheis Dé go raibh a h-anam dílis.

Geraldine Fitzgerald
(Little Company of Mary)

Our Sr Eucharia was a very special person. It was a wonderful day when she came into our lives and I know I speak also for my late husband, Johnny. With her love and prayers, she taught us to know and love Jesus, our Lord and Saviour. I remember thinking that I knew God because I feared him, but Eucharia taught me to pray to a loving God, with the result that I began to know and to love others as I should. That was almost thirty years ago.

To be in her company at prayer meetings and at social events was a great joy. I will never forget sharing her vegetable lasagne, which she taught me to cook. She prayed with me and for me on many occasions, helping me overcome all my fears. I have known and loved her since and always will. I will always remember her with a grateful and loving heart.

With much love.

Bridie Cooling
Shannon, Co. Clare

I was first introduced to Sr Eucharia in 1976. I was invited to my very first prayer meeting in a neighbour's house. This was very new to me and I felt confused to say the least. After a while I made my excuses and left. Later, there was a knock on my door. It was Sr Eucharia. 'Well', she said, 'how did you enjoy our meeting?' I looked at her and said, 'I think you are all mad!' She threw back her head and gave a hearty laugh and said, 'That's OK'. We chatted for a while as I felt quite comfortable in her company. Eucharia asked me to try the prayer meetings in the local hall for four weeks to see how I felt.

That for me was the start of a long road to God that has changed my outlook and prayer-life forever. I have a lot of lovely memories over the course of nearly twenty years: retreats in Spanish Point, spending time together in mass and prayer groups and, of course, the leisure time we all spent together, like sitting on the beach singing along to the guitar, and lots of laughter. The list goes on.

This lovely, caring woman gave so much of her time and self to every one; her motto was 'Keep it simple'.

My last memory of her was a visit to her home in Corofin, which she shared with her dear friend Sr Geraldine. Eucharia had baked lovely scones and, buoyed by many cups of tea, we spent the evening chatting – a lovely time.

Through this caring lady, loved by so many people, I met lots of good people who became life-long friends. I feel privileged to have known this little woman with a lovely smile and a big heart. God, I'm sure, is blessing and rewarding you now. Thank you, Eucharia, for lovely memories.

Carmel Diamond
Leeds, England

Be with God.
That is where I am,
not looking for anything
which I do not have already.

Eucharia! Eucharia was someone who was able to give you a sense of dignity despite, or almost because, you were struggling with problems. We met her when we were both struggling with mental illness. Mental illness is stigma-laden. It isolates you and makes you feel worthless. Eucharia helped us to see that it is in life's struggles that people are and become human.

She could be all in one; friend – full of celebration and humour; co-explorer – of ideas, of spirituality; co-mystic – facing the unknown. She was someone who delighted in you, and yet you knew she delighted in lots of people. Above all, she was generous and kind and would give advice if asked. It was because of her support that I risked going back to college at thirty-six to study psychology. Fran and I have both recovered. We had many loving hands and hearts helping us. Eucharia was there for us for many years.

Mike and Fran Watts
Kilkenny

We have one solid comfort amidst all this little tripping about: our hearts can always be in the same place, centred in God, for whom alone we go forward or stay back.

These words of Catherine McAuley, written in December 1840, speak to me of the Eucharia I knew. She too was often 'unsettled', and 'tripping about', in one sense of the phrase, was second nature to her.

She might not have agreed with me, but I always regarded Eucharia as the personification of all that was good about Mercy. She exuded a love of God that expressed itself in a passionate and practical concern for those who were experiencing pain in this world in whatever form. As a teacher of religion Eucharia was inspirational. Former pupils in Spanish Point and Ennis secondary schools still talk with affection of their experience of someone who held them enthralled as she introduced them to the gospels and to a spirituality based on a relationship with a loving God.

I remember Eucharia as someone who could 'talk for Ireland'! She held pupils and colleagues spellbound – sometimes when all should have been elsewhere – with that charismatic way of hers and a typical disregard for regulation or regimentation. Many a time in the community dining room we stood for grace after meals, ready to go back to the task of the day when one by one we sat again because Eucharia was holding forth on some topic or other! As a newly qualified teacher I joined her in the Home Economics faculty of Coláiste Muire – she was welcoming, supportive, encouraging and open to new ideas. It was at this time that she shared with me a hurt she carried through her life: her training as a Home Economics teacher, while accredited, had been acquired part-time over a series of summer courses. At a time of teacher shortage, many trained this way. I always felt that she was one of those in religious life whom community had failed by not providing them the opportunity for a full-time, professional preparation for life in the classroom.

Eucharia was a natural and well-read philosopher and theologian. She also had that saving sense of humour that highlighted the funny side of life. I remember spending hours with her plucking snipe – a gift from her brother, Fr Jim, after a day's fowling – and amidst the feathers and the laughter she said she wished he had found other recipients as we might as well be plucking sparrows! This was an easy cue for pondering the 'sparrows of the field' and God's providence. Her trust in people was sometimes misplaced – as on the day she was completely taken in by a 'nun' questing at the convent door for money to help build a church in the Ukraine. A letter, proffered as proof of genuineness, had been written that same day by the Bishop. Eucharia gave away our entire petty cash for the rest of the month – the princely sum of two pounds! Not a lot by today's standard. She declared at supper that she had met a true follower of the Lord – she had 'seen Christ in her eyes'. Within the hour there was a visit from the Gardaí who were searching for a certain foreign gentleman masquerading as a nun! She was not the first to be conned – this time she was in the company of a bishop – nor would she be the last. She could laugh at that experience while hoping that it wouldn't ever cause her to refuse help to anyone else.

When Eucharia left teaching to work with the traveller community and to set up what was to grow into Clare Social Services she left a void in Mercy education and in our community at Coláiste Muire that could never be filled. She had already shown signs of her interest in being closer to those who were experiencing economic and family difficulties by holding evening classes for some women from the town in basic cookery and money management. These classes were small and often turned into counselling sessions. We were sad to see her go but recognised her restless spirit and her desire to blaze a different trail – but Eucharia was not satisfied with a single new trail! She blazed many.

How often did I think, 'this is it, she has found what she's looking for', only to meet Eucharia and hear of a new dream, a new quest for solitude and contemplation that always led to the inevitable encounter with others to talk about the God of love, and to a sharing mixed with prayer. Only days before her death in McAuley House, in a barely audible voice, Eucharia spoke of prayer – she had come through a dark and difficult time, to once more radiating a conviction about God's love expressed in the ordinary.

A random selection of incidents comes to mind as I recall my relationship with Eucharia. She often called me her 'rescuer' – as in the time she had bravely gone to work in Ballyfermot while Sr Caoimhin (Little Sister of the Assumption) took a sabbatical. The prospect of being an advocate in court for young men in trouble appealed to her – but she was ill prepared for the reality of her home being burgled by some of the people she was helping. She was so frightened on the phone that I said I would come and collect her. There was no resistance as this mission came to a premature end and we loaded up the car with her meagre, personal belongings – which, to my surprise, included cake tins and queen-cake tins and other kitchen utensils. Caring and baking for others was part of who Eucharia was.

Those who knew Eucharia knew of her constant hankering after the contemplative. I once took her to a hermitage in Co. Waterford; she had found the 'ideal place of solitude and simplicity'. Instinctively I knew it would not last and was not surprised when the offer of a 'lift' home was soon welcomed – another 'rescue'!

There were the times she shared a caravan in Kilfenora, her departure for Inis Oírr, her sojourn with the Mercies in London, working in a night shelter, and with an order of enclosed, contemplative Sisters in Wexford. I recall a visit to Eucharia one night in a house called 'Greenbrier' in Limerick where she ran a half-way house for men from the psychiatric hospital – she and they were kneeling at kitchen chairs saying the rosary. It was a sacred time. An atmosphere of peace, respect and of being in a safe, caring environment was palpable. I came home convinced that this was going to be a long-term mission. Within months Eucharia was requested to go to Kilrush to a newly formed community in John Paul Estate. And then there was Corofin where she found a very special community – where she loved and was loved, where the sharing of bread, friendship and prayer were as natural as breathing. That love sustained her for more than twenty years of life and welcomed her back in the most extraordinary way in death and kept vigil with her to the end.

For Eucharia 'all this tripping around' has ended. She and Catherine McAuley are both at home, 'centred in God' – a life-long ambition for both of them at last fulfilled. I thank God for her life, for the privilege of knowing her and for belonging to a Mercy congregation that can accommodate diversity of giftedness.

Sr Canice Hanrahan, RSM

A dream:
people
who because of some experience
of the 'Allness',
of God and of his love
are willing to let go of many things,
people for whom God is the only absolute
and who, therefore, hold all his gifts loosely.

Season of Mellow Fruitfulness

In the beginning of the year,
there is a snowdrop,
a crocus, some daffodils and tulips.
Then,
when summer comes,
there can be gardens, full of flowers.
But in the autumn
God just empties out his paintbox everywhere
for everybody to enjoy.

Sr Eucharia! A book in her memory is a wonderful idea and so she will live on, not only in the hearts of those she touched, but through the written word as well.

While I cannot claim her as a friend, I met Sr Eucharia on a few occasions and always came away greatly enriched. Just being in her presence, I sensed a deeper presence radiating through her as she poured herself into my soul. She was on fire with the love of Jesus.

She told me about her new venture – going to the village of Corofin to live in the midst of the people in a small house that would always have an open door and a welcome for whoever chose to visit.

On many occasions, a Legion of Mary friend, Paddy O'Sullivan, gave some glowing accounts of that 'little nun' who was doing so much good.

Through her life of deep prayer she passed on that sense of prayer to others. Little prayer groups were formed. She reached out to so many, all throughout her lifetime.

On 24 March 2005 she took a 'non-stop flight' to heaven and we treasure her memory in our hearts.

Ada Power
Clare Castle

Why did you go to Corofin?
The first thing that comes to mind
was the stillness, inside and outside,
and meeting people didn't break it.

Eucharia! Where would one start? I feel that anything I write would not do justice to this woman. Of course I can just imagine her amazement if she thought that anyone was writing anything at all. This was a big part of her secret, I think – her humility.

She didn't fit into any box; boxes are enclosed things and she couldn't be fenced in by anything. The only labels to describe her are compassionate, inspiring, loving, caring, considerate, generous, humorous. She would say she was a woman first and then a nun; she was an ordinary woman with an extraordinary life. So I ask myself how does the ordinary and the extraordinary become one. I think for Eucharia it was by allowing the Spirit of God to work through her and to guide her life totally.

While living in Corofin, Eucharia was very much a part of the community and of its families. She visited a lot of homes, both socially and wherever there was any need: a new-born baby, sickness, death, poverty or whatever. People always said they felt uplifted after she had called. One person's comment was that when she visited her home, her teenage children, who usually made themselves quite scarce when other adults came, would gather all around her. We feel privileged that she visited us so frequently in our own home. She used to say she loved to come into a family situation. She loved to get involved with children. She would always have a space for them, whether it was reading a book or answering some burning questions. They always loved to see her coming and would announce her with delight by saying 'Oh! Eucharia is coming'. They saw her as very special.

She often spoke about the fact that her own brothers and sisters didn't marry and that, therefore, she did not have an experience of life within a family. So that, I think, is why she was at times in awe of things that she would see in ours. Not that there was anything extraordinary to experience. But what she found so wonderful was watching us just playing with a child or giving them a hug when they were hurt or looking after them when they were sick. She could see God in all these ordinary actions. Then, of course, she made it possible for us to see that everything we did in the family resembled how God cares for us who are his own.

She also helped us to reflect on scripture and for me that was a totally new approach to prayer. It has enriched my life enormously. I now attempt to share this with some others through the two prayer meetings we attend and which she began. She helped me to relate in prayer to God as to a loving friend, and seeing God as such gave me the freedom to just speak to him in my own words, as I would to Donal [her husband]; as a result I began to pray spontaneously and with much more ease.

Moreover, when I talked to her about some areas of faith that puzzled me, Eucharia always seemed to recognise exactly where I was and wisely guided me. She seemed so sure in her own faith that others always looked to her for help. She was constantly in touch with God's own Spirit as she spoke, and consequently she drew people to herself, although she did once make an effort to be alone with God by going to Inis Oírr. She thought that her plan to be alone would be successful! When she told me, I just laughed. 'Why did you laugh', she asked. I said, 'That just won't happen, Eucharia'. She replied that it would but two weeks later her first letter said, 'Guess what? When I was coming out of mass today a woman stopped to talk to me. She asked me if I would begin a prayer meeting on the island'. That lady obviously sensed that Eucharia had something special. This is difficult to describe. I think it was the Christ in her, but if it was, he always forced her to give up her dreams to follow God's own plan.

When our grandchildren heard that Eucharia had died they decided to give her a good send-off, as they saw it. They made a little arrangement with stones and flowers from the garden and held a ritual of their own. They were overheard praying for her: 'Holy God, take Eucharia to heaven quickly and don't forget the flowers, as she loved flowers and we want her to have flowers in heaven'. Nobody knew this was happening and the children had not been prompted by adults. Thank God somebody passed and heard this. Eucharia gave so much to children.

A symbol that describes her life for me is that of a living vessel from which God's love flows continuously. It is never empty, because all the time Eucharia spent in prayer keeps it topped up.

Eucharia, may you rest in peace.

Maura Cleary
Corofin

Draw me.
When you do, everything else fades into nothingness
and only the longing remains.
And when you go away?
Yes, there is only faith left and trust.

My first encounter with Sr Eucharia was when I attended an adult religious course in Ennis that she gave. It consisted of one night per week for the six weeks of Lent, and her main topic was 'Our image of God and our relationship with God'. Eucharia would often say that, if her image of God was as described by some people (and she gave various examples), she wouldn't have anything to do with God either!

What Eucharia did for most of us was that she shared her faith in God, her image of God, her own relationship with God and her knowledge of God's love for each and every one of us. Eucharia was like a farmer feeding his young calf from a bucket. By giving the calf a taste of the milk in the bucket it would follow him around the field or wherever he would like to lead it. Eucharia had the good food and she kept on giving us a taste and working up in us a hunger and a great desire for more.

Eucharia used every opportunity to draw people closer to God. I remember one night when we were getting our young child ready for bed. He had fallen asleep and Eucharia watched as we, his parents, carefully took off one set of clothes and carefully put on another. Then I noticed one small tear running down her cheek. She later said that she was overcome by how God cared for that little child. As parents we were only doing what so many parents do for their own child but through Eucharia we gained a sense of the spiritual dimension of our actions: we had been God's hands for that little child, and can be in so many other areas of ordinary daily living.

Eucharia opened us up to listen to the scriptures. I remember how, at some of her earlier prayer meetings, she would teach us how to quieten down and let prayer happen. Sometimes she would use a fantasy story and invite us to allow some symbol to arise and then to listen carefully to what it was suggesting for our lives. During prayer she would have us spend time reflecting on a passage from the scriptures and to find in it some message which would be appropriate for here and now. Eucharia would always offer us an opportunity to share that message, if we wished.

Rather than teaching us how to pray, Eucharia herself prayed in our presence and when she did that she could not hide her own deep, beautiful relationship with the Lord. Eucharia constantly walked with God in everything she said and did and saw and heard; she was always on the road to Emmaus. She journeyed with us and at times our hearts would burn within us as she talked.

Jesus, Eucharia's friend, the Lord whom Eucharia knew and loved so well, is now our own friend and our Lord. Our image of what God is has been changed because of Eucharia's stay in our village of Corofin.

May God bless her and may she delight in him forever, as she experiences his delight in her. Eucharia often quoted from scripture, 'In you, my love is my delight ... I have called you by name, you are mine and I love you'. Eucharia has helped us to believe those words.

Donal Cleary
Corofin

There was a small house going at the time. It was
near the chapel. I felt I wanted to get away. That
was always in me, the quiet and the time for prayer.
I suppose I should have entered a Contemplative Order.
When I was a novice, I said it to a priest who said:
'You are where God wants you to be.' I made
another effort and Bishop Rodgers said to leave it
for a while. It never happened.

I used to talk to Sr Eucharia when she came to visit Maura
[Cleary]. I remember that she always had a cup of tea and a chat
with Maura and was always very nice to us (me and Diarmuid).
She was a lovely woman and seemed always to have sweets for us.
She even made things for us at Christmas. I used to talk to Sr
Eucharia over the wall of my house. She loved to hear what I was
doing. I have a lovely holy water font that she gave to my Mam
when she came to visit her after I was born. It's very special to me.
She had a sort of presence that no one else had.

Mary Ellen Nagle (aged ten)
Corofin

Our first meeting with Sr Eucharia was filled with trepidation,
doubt and even disbelief. How could a seventy-year-old nun
understand marriage and family life?

We had done a weekend for married couples called 'Marriage
Encounter' and we had follow-up monthly meetings where we

discussed various aspects of family life. It was then suggested that we turn our monthly meetings into prayer nights with Sr Eucharia as facilitator.

Her emphasis on living out family life based on the scriptures was something that we struggled with at first, but gradually 'the seeds were sown'. Eucharia persevered and enlightened us with her own personal insights into the scriptures, and she was able to bring out their relevance in today's busy world.

The next 'move' was to get us to host prayer nights in our homes – in other words, to lead those who arrived with scripture reading and in prayer. This made us squirm. We felt totally inadequate and incompetent for such a task. But with encouragement from Eucharia and, no doubt, with guidance from the Holy Spirit, this in fact has come to pass. Donal and Maura Cleary hosted the first night and, with a little prompting, we all took our turn. At these meetings we would try to share our thoughts and our reflections on the scriptures and then wait for the 'Eucharia bit'. She would give us her own particular slant – revealing her great understanding of the sacred scriptures. Again and again she emphasised that God loves each and every one of us and that he holds us in the palm of his hand.

We now look forward to these monthly prayer nights in our homes and the sharing of our faith has been a great support to us and to our families. We still meet once a month and while there is an empty chair, we feel her presence and maybe the 'Eucharia bit' has now become part of our own sharing.

So the 'seeds' that were sown by Eucharia are living on in many groups in which she was involved – quite a legacy for a retired nun who set up house in Corofin over twenty years ago.

Sean and Mary McDermott
Ennis

We have to be people of prayer,
no matter what our ministry,
or we are sounding brass.

I first got to know Sister when I was very young and when she lived beside the Clare Heritage Museum in Corofin. She used to call me 'Tina'. She was a very kind-hearted, caring person; she had an understanding of the younger generation and I remember her as always being happy!

My two friends and I used to visit her almost every day. She would invite us in and give us sweets, which she had bought up the street that morning. While on our visit, we would listen to stories about Jesus and his twelve apostles. She would tell the stories in a way that we, at the age of six or seven, could appreciate and understand.

I remember that on Saturdays we used to help her make some buns and, while we would be waiting for the buns to bake, she would put on a video of Jesus. Upstairs there was a room known to me and to my friends as the 'Jesus Room'. We used to paint pictures and pick flowers and every time we visited we would go up to that room with more paintings and more flowers. I think that in the end she had to store them in a different place because the room was soon so full.

Sister also taught us how to knit. So, frequently, we would go down for a lesson on how to make a scarf. When she told us about the people in the 'third world' we soon gathered all our old clothes, shoes and toys and made our way down to her house beside the river to give the clothes to the children in the poorer countries. She was very thoughtful like that. I remember her making scarves and hats for these people. I can still imagine her sitting on her chair by the fireplace, knitting, the wool piled up on the table across from her.

I also remember once when a group of young kids from my neighbourhood got together and put on a small show in our community hall, St Patrick's. The show was called 'Fr Ted', and we had a song by The Spice Girls which we performed at the beginning of our show. Sister came to our rehearsals and to our 'opening night'. I could tell that she enjoyed herself by her laugh!

When she fell ill, my friend and I, along with her mother, went to visit her in the Cahercalla Hospital, but she had been discharged earlier that day. The last time I heard her name was when she had passed on. I cannot describe how I felt; shock, sadness – it was something I couldn't believe.

A vigil was held for her in St Brigid's Church, so my two friends and I went along for a couple of hours, to see her one last time. We remembered all the times we baked buns, knitted, heard stories about Jesus and just talked about ourselves and school!

There will never be anyone who could ever replace her. She is greatly missed by the people of Corofin and by me and by my friends. We will always remember her.

Christina Linnane
Corofin

I hoped to live a simple life without any trappings,
a simple Christian life, back to the Gospel.
Christ didn't cut himself away, he was a carpenter.
Poor and rich were all the same.
He had nowhere to lay his head.
To live the simplest life possible,
true simplicity and the people.

When I think of Eucharia I think, rather greedily, of her delicious cooking. I remember the first time Emer, Veronica and I went to Corofin – to the old house which I associate with her the most. She made a delicious pork and apricot dish and did something with cream, mayonnaise and baked potatoes. That was many years ago now but it has stayed with me. I think I remember the cooking because it was symbolic of how grounded Eucharia was. She had an 'of the earth', rooted, essential quality to her and her spirituality was of that kind too. She did not have an airy or ascetic spirituality – it was very solid and warm and homely and real, which was such a strength.

Another thing I associate with Eucharia is a story she told me about psycho-synthesis. She recalled doing an exercise where you walked in your imagination through a forest and saw a house. Different people would come out, each representing sub-personalities of oneself. Lots of people met quite a crowd coming out of the house! Eucharia told me how she met just one person – herself.

Eucharia told me that story quite a few years ago and it has always summed up for me who I met when I met Eucharia. She was always herself; there were no other parts, no differences, and I think I have never met anyone else who had that quality to such a degree.

More recently I remember visiting Eucharia in the convent in Ennis, shortly before she went to Limerick. She was asking about everybody and became quite confused as I told her. I was upset at first and tried to clarify everything for her but then I realised that it did not matter: confused or alert she was still the same person. The essence of Eucharia was as real and as grounded and as warm as it had ever been.

At her funeral in Corofin it felt very good to have Veronica and Emer there also – like a return to where we started out from and a chance to renew.

Máire Kennedy
Newmarket on Fergus

What meant so much to me was the fact that I could call and tell Eucharia everything and she'd listen in the context of faith. She affirmed in me my ability as a priest and convinced me that I have a real gift with people in a parish. I see priesthood as a ministry of friendship and so the Church is everywhere. When I look at the people before me at mass, I try to be aware of their struggles and pain, and feel it's a great thing that they gather in a human way. If I can connect their struggles with the Eucharist, then they can go home with a bit of hope. This is the highlight of my week, to be with the people celebrating the Eucharist. I don't judge families who don't attend mass. I called to one such family, a man, his wife and two children and with them I was certain I was in the presence of the whole Church, thanks to Eucharia.

Eucharia helped me in the following ways:

- She started me on a path of growth which I have pursued. I now have someone to accompany me on my journey. All this has helped me to grow as a person and has convinced me that the closer one comes to oneself, the closer one comes to God.
- She helped me appreciate the psalms.
- She helped me use the breviary in my own way.
- She freed me to trust my instincts and go along with whatever happens and let go of senses of obligation to duties if the needs of people dictate it.
- Our formation as priests in the past left a lot to be desired and didn't trust our deep personal knowledge / wisdom / conscience. It was my opinion, and Eucharia's, that it was too focused on Canon Law.
- Above all she helped me see that at the level of parish I had a lot to give. As a student, and always, I was drawn to silent prayer. She saw that in me and she drew it out (*'educare'*) and convinced me that I had great gifts for priesthood.

Eucharia poured out love wherever she went.

A Priest

A Spirit in my Life
We, the people of Corofin, County Clare were blessed to have Sr Eucharia among us for many years. Sr Eucharia had eyes and ears for everyone, regardless of age, colour or creed. A person of the greatest understanding and wisdom!

Her belief in God and in the power of prayer was the greatest part of her giving. Whenever she spoke, this flowed from her, never forceful, just there. Her love for God and life she shared with all. The good part of everyone, she could always find. Even in the most difficult situation where I would have to struggle to find it, she had it found, spot on! She was a great believer in life in the Spirit. This is something which inspired me and the hymn 'Spirit of the Living God, fall afresh on us', sang often at our prayer group meetings, reminds me that God is always present and can help us at all times.

Sr Eucharia's sharp eyes, her patiently listening ear, her words of wisdom and her faith is her legacy left to all of us. I thank God for the privilege of having been here in her time.

Christine Kearney
Corofin

We are here for the people
who are welcome at our house
at any hour of the day or night.

I had the pleasure of meeting Sr Eucharia in the early 1980s, shortly after I moved to the Corofin area from Dublin with my family. I found her interesting to talk to and, at her invitation, sometimes called to her for morning coffee. When one is new to an area it is always enjoyable to meet someone who shares some of your interests. I discovered that Sr Eucharia and I had the same interest in certain books and we would sometimes compare notes on our readings and interpretations of a particular book.

She had a great sense of humour and many were the amusing incidents from our lives which we exchanged. I would not necessarily have always agreed with her point of view, but she was a wonderful listener and the great love she had for our Lord and Saviour Jesus Christ was obvious. On a number of occasions she gave cookery demonstrations to some young boys and girls from the village, one of them being one of my daughters, then aged ten or eleven. Whilst the goodies were baking she would chat with them and after would share out the eagerly awaited buns. This took patience and generosity on her part and to me it was the gospel in action.

She was a rock of good sense and would have dismissed any notion of being missed after her death. I am sure that Our Lord and Our Lady would agree that she made good use of her time here on this earth.

Bernadette Byrne
Corofin

We rarely forget that which made a deep impression on our minds.
Tyron Edwards

Sr Eucharia is someone who will always be in the minds of everybody she taught. During her days in Corofin, Eucharia loved to see children playing and enjoying themselves and would always stop to have a chat with them. I remember Eucharia when, as children of four or five, a group of us would regularly visit her down at the end of Bridge Street – the house with the 'glass ball' in the middle window. She would welcome us little lunatics into her home and have lovely home-made scones and little sandwiches ready for us with tea and some fizzy drinks. She would then give us pictures to colour and we would stick them on the wall for her. She treasured these, as they were the work of children.

I was fortunate that, from the age of one, until I was twelve, Maura Cleary was my babysitter and Eucharia was a regular caller to Maura's house. She would love coming out to the back of the house to play with the other children and myself until Maura would call us in for dinner. She would ask about our exciting day in school and show great interest in all that we had learned and in what we, little kids, had to say.

Sr Eucharia was a very kind and helpful lady. Her life was full of happiness and smiles and she would always make you laugh when she visited your home. She had a special gift when people had a tragedy in their lives in that she would listen to their story and give them great encouragement.

I remember when Eucharia was told that she had to move into a house in Ennis and leave Corofin for good. This was a big shock for her and, of course, for the people of Corofin. I had not seen her for a few years until one day she called to our home. I opened the door to welcome her in but I was saddened and shocked to see how fragile she had got in such a short time. She immediately asked me how I was, and what I had been doing, and if I was dancing still? I told her that I was and she praised my commitment to Irish dancing and said how wonderful I was.

Eucharia will always have a special place in my heart and she will never be forgotten. She has taught us so much over the years while she lived in Corofin. She made an impact on the lives of all of us who now are in our teenage years, in secondary schools and colleges, and getting ready for the challenges of the world.

Thank you, Eucharia, for such lovely memories.

Edel Lahiffe
Corofin

I never found that people interfered with my prayer life;
it was the opposite.
Their lives and unselfishness were an example to me.
I was a good neighbour with a 'Jesus Room',
as the children called it.

The Face of my Living God
In November 1983, Eucharia Keane came into my life and became for me my 'She-God'. I had just had a miscarriage. I miscarried my son at eighteen weeks into the pregnancy, and was devastated. Within three weeks I was seriously ill in hospital with no diagnosis.

Living in Corofin with one of our dear friends, Sr Geraldine Collins, was Eucharia. Eucharia heard my cries for help to the Lord and she told Geraldine that she would visit me. I had an eighteen-month old daughter, Sinead, and a lovely husband and I so wanted to live and to be well. That's how I met Eucharia.

I learned the following from Eucharia:

• She loved Jesus passionately and was present to him in every single moment of her life.
• She encouraged me to commit myself to the Lord through my prayer life and encouraged my involvement with a prayer group which I attended. Eucharia, however, was very clear that a prayer group should never be 'a holy huddle'. She was clear that the relationship we have with the Lord must be put into action every single day and in every situation.
• As Eucharia often said, 'God has only got our hands, our ears and our spirit to show his love in the world'.

I spent some time with Eucharia prior to her going out to Inis Oírr where she desired to be alone with God. Yet I know that, during her time there, people came to her, and Jesus used Eucharia in his own way to call those people to himself through her.

As Eucharia got older she could have retired to one of the bigger convents or to a nursing home. However, her spirit and the Lord's wish for her was that she stay in Corofin. She was so thrilled when her Mercy Community heard her voice and facilitated her remaining there.

We all know the contribution that Eucharia made to the people of Corofin over the next eleven years. Had her community not heard her voice and God's will for her, it would have been a tragedy and an absolute lost opportunity for hundreds of people.

As Eucharia's health deteriorated, it was obvious that she was slowly returning to her first and only love, the Lord. I received the gift of sharing some of my life's journey with Eucharia, and in the words of the song, composed by Breege O'Hare OSE, 'How Wonderful is My Soul', Eucharia's spirit and how she loved the Lord is aptly represented:

How wonderful is my soul which you, my God, have created;
Nothing can truly show its beauty,
Nothing can truly set me free,
Except your love flowing through my being,
Speaking to me of things unknown,
And in your Love flowing through my being,
My soul awakens to you, Holy One.

Ann Byrne
Galway

Sr Eucharia! She was a wonderful person, whose love affair with God/Divinity was inspirational. Love/Divinity flowed through her, regardless of the situation she was in.

Through her example, she invited others to find the divinity within them. She touched so many hearts with her love. I am grateful for having known and loved her and am happy as I feel that she has now more freedom in her present spirit-form and that she consequently will continue to express her love and the divinity to us.

Thank you, Eucharia. Thank you, God.

A Friend

As a teacher Eucharia had no peer. Her gentleness, kindness and love of the Lord shone through in all her dealings with us.

I have very fond memories of her as a next-door neighbour. She was just the tonic for me as I went through a very difficult patch in life because of illness and of big decisions that I had to make. Eucharia prayed both with and for me and, being so close to the Lord, her prayers were always answered in the most amazing ways. Her great sense of fun always surfaced at the right time.

A walk with Eucharia in Dromore Wood was a wonderful experience. She could name every tree and shrub. In fact, she had a great love of nature and a trip to the Burren lifted her spirits and the spirits of all who had the privilege of being with her.

Eucharia moved house in Corofin but still continued to visit me every Sunday night. I shall always treasure the memories of those visits. I can honestly say she gave me a great love of the Eucharist.

Of course Eucharia was Christ-like in every way. She loved the young (and they loved her); she loved the old, the rich and everybody who was poor. Her knowledge of the Bible had to be heard to be believed. She had a wonderful memory and often quoted poetry she had learned at primary school; her knowledge of history was outstanding.

She once told me a story about the chimney sweep who came to her to do some work. She was recovering from a broken leg at the time and he said to her, 'You're lucky you're not a horse or you'd have had to be shot'! She laughed about that comment for days. She had such a wonderful sense of humour and really enjoyed a good joke.

Eucharia's final illness was so sad. We all knew she was going to the Lord. On one of my last visits to her she said, 'We'll all be together again with the Lord'. I am firmly convinced Eucharia is now a saint and I pray daily to her – not for her.

Lena Macnamara
Corofin

The Church can only change
when the people are allowed
to participate fully.

The evening that Sr Eucharia and Sr Geraldine came to live next door to me, I went out to welcome them. I was doing a job in my back yard and was determined not to delay. Eucharia asked if I would wait for the prayer meeting, which was about to start. I said that I couldn't as I was in the middle of a job. She just said, 'maybe some other time'. I then left to continue with my work. Now there are only about twenty yards between our two front doors. Before I reached my own door I had changed my mind. I turned back to the prayer meeting, greeted by a smile and a hug from Eucharia. That was the beginning of many years of friendship. I don't think I ever missed a prayer meeting while Eucharia was in Bridge Street.

That story is to prove the effect that she had on everyone she spoke to; you knew straight away when you met her that you were talking to someone very special.

My wife had died so we decided to help each other, and that was what we did. I had a car so I made her promise that she would let me know if she ever wanted to go somewhere. I took her into Ennis to visit her doctor, her dentist, into the convent and to the bus. She had a sister in Dublin whom she visited on a regular basis. I would take her to Ennis to meet the Dublin bus on a Tuesday and I would meet her in Ennis on her return on Friday. This went on for years. Then her sister sold her house and moved to a nursing home in Blackrock, in Cork. I took her down there a few times to see her.

Now I am going to tell you an incident that happened one Friday, just to let you know how close she was to God. Her usual bus arriving from Dublin came in at 2.10 p.m. Of course I was there waiting for it. Eucharia was not on it. Two more buses came and she was not on them. I waited until 2.30 p.m. Everybody had left at this stage so I decided to go home. I felt there would be a message on my phone from her. I came over by the Friary and right at the gate there was a parking space; it struck me that it was an ideal time to get confession. I went in, got confession, came out and sat into the car. While I was buckling my seat belt, the thought struck me, 'Should I go back to the station again? Maybe she's coming on a later bus?' As I drove into the station, Eucharia was walking down the steps from the ticket office. I picked her up and when she sat into the car the tears came to her eyes. She looked across at me and she said, 'Frank, I came and saw nobody here. I asked God to send Frank back, so here you are'.

It was not all a one-sided affair. Eucharia was very good to me. Any advice I wanted, she gave to me. She was a great cook and was always making nice things, but she made two of everything, one for Geraldine and herself and one for Frank. She had me spoilt. Apart from holiness, there was another side to her. She had a great sense of humour. There was a party at Jimmy Lahiffe's one night. Geraldine and Eucharia went in Geraldine's car, and I went in my own sometime later. About midnight Geraldine said that Eucharia was getting tired so I said I would take her home, which I did. We got out of the car and I walked to the door with her and waited until she was inside. She turned the key in the door and opened it, then turned around and with a smile she said, 'Do you know, Frank, you're the first man ever to take me home from a dance'!

When she moved into Ennis I took her out to Corofin every Monday night to the prayer meetings, and back again. It meant a lot to her as she loved Corofin. She often said that being there was the happiest time of her life. Before she died, my friend Nora, her little grandchild of four and I visited her nearly every week while she was in the nursing home in Limerick. She loved to hear all the news from Corofin.

When she died, her remains were taken to Corofin church for a night. The funeral was met outside her own house in Bridge Street by a guard of honour and conveyed to the church. After a most beautiful ceremony the remains were left lying with the coffin uncovered in front of the altar until 2.00 p.m. the following day.

The way she was adored by the people of Corofin was borne out by the number of people who paid their respects all during the night and the following day until the remains were removed into the convent at 2.00 p.m. I know because to say my sincere thanks to her for all her goodness to me I sat by her coffin from 8.00 p.m. that evening until 2.00 p.m. the following day. She is now reaping her reward with God.

Frank Fitzpatrick
Corofin

My first encounter with the late Sr Eucharia was in Corofin church in 1990. I was not long home from London, after over fifty years. On entering the church I took a seat in front of the altar, only to be told by a lady in the church that Mrs 'So and So' sits there. I tried another; same response. It was then that Sr Eucharia stood up and said 'come to my seat', adding that there are no reservations in God's home.

When Sr Eucharia moved to Bridge Street I met her more frequently. Many times she asked me in for a cup of coffee or for a chat. Sister was a very interesting nun; she was full of knowledge and was good to everyone in Corofin who looked for guidance or advice.

To anybody who was sick or who had lost a loved one, she gave comfort and whatever help she could. She also organised some cookery classes in St Patrick's Hall and taught young mothers how to make up simple dinners. Apart from that she was involved in Clare Care and she pioneered the holiday home in St Joseph's Convent in Lahinch where elderly people from all over Co. Clare would come on five-day breaks. I myself have attended for the past five years. If this home had not been there a lot of elderly folk would never have experienced a holiday by the sea.

She had a rare gift of making people feel very special. On a personal note, I had a serious eye operation in a Cork hospital in 2000. She had no means of contacting me but went to a lot of trouble to discover who my neighbours were and then contacted them to offer help. I always hold that gesture very dear and much appreciated it.

Sister came with us to Knock and on all our many pilgrimages. She is gone now but she is not forgotten.

Ar Dheis Dé go raibh a h-anam dilis.

Bridie Malone
Corofin

The people are the Church.
We have to listen to them
and involve them fully.

To the best of my knowledge, Sr Eucharia came to Corofin in 1981. Having seen her at various functions and having met her at church and in the street, my first personal meeting with her occured in 1990. We had discussed holding a harvest mass and, because I knew that the celebration of harvesting had been for long associated with the Anglican Church and was not a Catholic tradition, I sought her advice. She was very enthusiastic about it and immediately involved herself with the preparation of the liturgy. Sr Eucharia was anxious to include a prayer of gratitude 'for all that gave life to the parish in the previous year', and not just for the produce of the soil. So the framework was set for future years and the harvest mass became an eagerly awaited annual event.

Sr Eucharia fully embraced life here in the village in all its aspects. She showed great interest in the raising of funds for the sporting facilities in the village, always willing to help and even to become a regular contributor to the lotto, drawn each week. Indeed, any project to do with the betterment of the village had her interest and involvement.

Sr Eucharia's attributes in both the spiritual and temporal spheres were many and varied. She was a woman blessed with many qualities:

- A great sense of humour.
- A tremendous faith, marked with a great devotion to the Eucharist and to Our Blessed Lady.
- Love of the countryside and the environment.

- The ability to listen.
- The gift of being hospitable. Her house was open to one and all, to young and old, to poor and well-to-do, to settled people and to travellers.
- The ability to offer sound advice to those in need. So often this advice would end with the words, 'Let us leave this now in the hands of God'.
- Organisational skills, reflected in her weekly prayer meetings. These were times of reflection and oral prayer. All needs of the parish were remembered. She also held sessions for the children, sometimes baking a cake as she prayed with them.

When she sustained an injury by a fall, the Sisters of Mercy decided that she should come back to Ennis to live. This was a decision that would cause her much distress, but faithful to her vow of obedience, she returned. She missed village life desperately. Shortly after her return she became ill and never recovered. Indeed, I often wonder if we had foreseen that she would be transferred would we have made arrangements which would have enabled her to stay in Corofin with us. But that was not to be, and when I went to see her in the hospital she talked about her yearning for the village and the people, but she added that she now was 'waiting for her God to come for her'.

May she rest in peace; our world in Corofin is much poorer for her passing.

Willie and Kathleen Corbett
Liscullane

Eucharia! Where could one begin or, for that matter, finish when remembering her? I think the thing I treasure most about her was her sense of humour, her laugh, her smile and her great gift of prayer. Eucharia showed us that prayer was joyful and even great fun! Many a prayer meeting ended up with as much laughter as prayer. 'God has a sense of humour too', she always said. Eucharia taught us not only how to pray but also how to listen to the Lord, to understand how he speaks to us through the scriptures and indeed through nature, music and the people we meet.

It wasn't only for these things that Eucharia was a blessing. We went to her for everything, from a pin to a recipe. Indeed, all problems, worries, questions, every joy and sorrow – she was there to listen, to advise and to give comfort. 'Bring it before the Lord', she would say, 'and I will pray for you too'. What more could we ask for?

Eucharia, we miss you, we love you and we will never forget you.

Mena Lahiffe
Corofin

I only want to be a good neighbour,
not a representative of the official Church.

We really came to know Sr Eucharia when she joined our rosary prayer group in Corofin in the late nineties. We used to meet on Tuesday nights to pray and to recite the rosary. Her prayerfulness and insight into the gospels sometimes left me speechless, and we were always richer for her presence among us. Before the night ended with a cup of tea we would have had many a laugh as her wonderful humour knew no bounds.

We will forever remember Eucharia as a deeply spiritual, warm, good-humoured lady with a deep, deep love for the Eucharist. We know she is home now with her Beloved and looking down on all of us with deep affection. We will never forget you, Eucharia.

Willie, Eileen and Stephen Lahiffe
Corofin

There is no life – no life without its hunger,
Each restless heart beats so imperfectly,
But when you come and I am filled with wonder,
Sometimes I think I glimpse Eternity.

These lyrics are from the popular song 'You Raise Me Up' and, for me, they speak volumes of the influence Sr Eucharia had on my life. My heart was restless, desperately seeking something. One cold, frosty Sunday evening I 'stumbled' across Sr Eucharia at evening prayer at the Poor Clare Monastery in Ennis and she invited me to her prayer meeting in Corofin, to 'come and see' for myself. Thank God, I accepted her invitation and over the next few years I was privileged to witness her deep, personal relationship with the Lord and to absorb the wisdom and the insights that she shared.

In leading us in prayer and contemplation, she helped us to glimpse eternity. A piece of scripture, a reading, a song or a picture was used to bring us to the Lord as she invited us to ponder its deep meaning in the silence and in the well-spring of our hearts. Afterwards she invited us to share our own experiences, if we wished, and the openness and honesty of those who did impressed me very much. I always came away with a beautiful sense of inner peace and calm.

She was anxious that the prayer groups would continue and encouraged us to take our turn in leading them so that we would be able to go out and bring good news to others.

Sr Eucharia was truly extraordinary. A very gifted woman and a wonderful teacher, she was always so humble and unassuming. She had a deep personal interest in everybody she encountered and she had empathy for those in trouble or in pain.

Surely the chorus of 'You Raise Me Up' summarises Sr Eucharia's message and legacy:

You raise me up so I can stand on mountains,
You raise me up to walk on stormy seas,
And I am strong when I am on your shoulders,
You raise me up to more than I can be.

Geraldine Carrigg
Ennis

While tending to Eucharia's house plant (*Sempervivum*), which was given with such happiness, we reflect on the fact that there were no obstacles to her generosity.

John and Kathleen O'Loughlin
Corofin

I first met Sr Eucharia in June 1992. At the time I wanted to rent a room for a local support group. On contact, it was as if we had known each other a lifetime. She surely was a phenomenal person in every way. Her sheer ability to listen, to comfort, to console, to reach out, to give especially to those in need, to the less well-off and to strugglers was second to none.

'Emmaus' house was hope-house. It was a house of prayer, love, peace and great joy for all. On leaving, one always felt that things would be OK as a result of being in her company. I suppose the one thing that would sum up this remarkable woman for me is the St Francis prayer: 'To be consoled, to be understood, to be loved.' I have never met anybody like her in my lifetime and I do not believe that I ever will again. Even though Eucharia no longer lives among us, I am aware that her spirit lives on and that she is near to every one of us and ready to intercede.

My family and I are proud to have known such a peace-loving woman as Eucharia. When trouble comes my way today, no matter in what shape or form, I think of 'Emmaus' house and of Eucharia. Then fond memories and the hope that I received from her come flooding back.

May Eucharia experience the joy of heaven as a reward for the love and joy that she so willingly gave to all on this earth.

Eternal rest grant to her, O Lord.

Gus O'Loughlin
Corofin

The Church needs to support family life.

We first met Sr Eucharia soon after our arrival here in 1993 and had very many positive conversations about her beliefs and work and our own parallel views on life.

There were daytime chats about everything and the greatly enjoyed Pensioners' Christmas Parties in Corofin, which Sr Eucharia attended, were always a positive experience.

We did very much miss the good lady when she retired to Ennis. For a very long time Sr Eucharia had been a fine part of the fabric of Corofin.

Marguerite and Mervyn Groves
Corofin

I first met Eucharia about ten years ago when Sr Geraldine brought her to my home. We struck up an instant rapport and shortly afterwards I visited her in Corofin. This was to be the first of many visits spread over the years, the last two or three being to the convent in Ennis. Looking back I regret that these visits were few and far between, but they were always a source of joy and reflection. I recall her greeting me with outstretched arms and a welcoming kiss before we sat down to put the world to rights! Our discussion ranged over many subjects, some political, some theological and some just plain gossip! Her respect for my Protestant views was always apparent and we could discuss the different aspects, not of faith because we both were members of the Christian Church, but of the petty ways in which faith is sometimes expressed. We argued and discussed and at the end we would agree on many things. What a pity that there are not more Eucharias so that we could all celebrate our similarities and at the same time both respect and understand our differences. My visits always ended with a cup of tea and home-made bread and cakes, in order to refresh the body, and a prayer to animate the soul.

There will never be another Eucharia; her openness and willingness to learn were always inspiring. Eucharia, I miss you, I pray for you and I know you are seated with your Lord and that with him you will be blessed for ever more.

Doreen Walker
Finavarra, Burren

Eucharia, a Woman of God and a True Friend to All
We feel very blessed that Eucharia chose to come and live among us in Corofin. She was truly a friend to everyone who crossed her door and she welcomed them with open arms, with tea and with a smile. Her unique take on life was an inspiration to all.

She had no interest in the materialistic side of life and was more likely to give your present away to someone who, in her eyes, was more deserving. She was always aware of the needy and nobody was ever turned away. She loved to give and the greatest gift she gave was her own love of God and of the scriptures. Her own understanding of the scriptures was profound and this she passed on to so many individuals.

Eucharia formed prayer groups for children and adults. The children loved to come to her and talk about their little problems, then to learn about the Lord through song and dance and prayer. People came from near and far to her for prayer and many had a change of heart, or even of career, because of their experience with Eucharia. She always encouraged younger people to remain at school and emphasised the importance of education. When a person was in pain or in a crisis she would say, 'Let's pray about it; God is over all; all will be well; love is all that matters in the end'.

Her counselling skills were well known and when people died in the parish, sometimes in tragic circumstances, she counselled and helped to explain even to the little ones the mysteries of life and death. Eucharia spent a lot of time praying in the little room at 'Emmaus' where the Blessed Sacrament was present. She was very much in favour of the participation of the laity in the Church and encouraged old and young to play an active role in Church affairs.

Eucharia took full part in community life in Corofin and loved to meet the people in the village. She enjoyed a joke and a laugh with them as she had a great sense of humour. She was famous for her cooking and shared her knowledge through cookery classes in the hall.

She also had a great love of nature. One time she discussed with a neighbour the fact that snails were eating her flowers. He recommended that she put out slug pellets to kill them. Her reply to this was, 'Oh no, I couldn't do that; they are God's creatures'. Eucharia loved all of God's creatures, big and small. Stray dogs often followed her down the street and she fed and cared for them until she could find them loving homes. The birds in her back garden were never short of a meal. An outing she looked forward to each May was to the most remote parts of the Burren to hear the cuckoo's call.

Eucharia, you will forever be remembered in the hearts and minds of those of us who have been blessed to know you. A person in Corofin, on hearing of Eucharia's death, said, 'We now have our very own saint in heaven'. Thank you, Eucharia, for your love, for your care and for the friendship that you offered to so many.

Go ndeana Dia trocaire ar a hanam uasal.

Mary O'Brien
Corofin

The example of married couples
has been an inspiration to my prayer.
I have learned about God's love
through what I have seen in ordinary family life:
a husband and wife who can be silent together,
a couple's care for their children.

I first met Eucharia when I was nine years old. She visited our home frequently and, as children, we visited her home for a children's prayer meeting. There we sang 'Joy, Joy, Joy' and 'His Banner over me is Love'. Beneath the smile of a sometimes quiet and retiring lady, one could glimpse the light of a deeper energy. Through the innocent eyes of a child, I viewed her as the norm for all. I later came to marvel at the love which was, through her, poured out on everyone.

Eucharia's life personified much of the road to Emmaus. She journeyed with so many people as they made their way on their own paths. She talked with people and she helped them to connect with deeper values, and so many of them consequently came to recognise a sacred presence in their midst as they broke bread together in their homes or in their parish church.

Eucharia's death touched all of us in a way that was profound, a fact that was expressed so wonderfully at her funeral. That final gathering was lead by many of her friends. It was testimony to her vision for the future of the Church: so many parts of just one body which combine to celebrate and to pass on the faith. It offered us the opportunity not just to grieve her passing, but to give thanks for a life as well, one which has now been taken up into the resurrection.

Leonard Cleary
Corofin

Ní rabhas ró-fhada im' phríomhoide i Scoil Mhuire Náisiúnta, Cora Finne nuair a chasadh orm don chéad uair riamh an tSiúr Eucharia. Chuir sí spéis mhór sa scoil agus sna páistí scoile agus go háirithe i ngach rud a bhain le cúrsaí chreidimh. Ba mhinic a bhuail sí isteach chugainn chun labhairt leo faoi scéalta ón mBíobla agus chun seirbhísí paidreoireachta a eagrú inár measc. Toisc gurbh bean cumasach, carthannach agus tuisceanach a bhí inti, chuaigh sí go mór i bhfeidhm ar na páistí. Le linn na seirbhísí sin chruthaigh sí atmaisféar draíochta nach bhféadfadh éinne a shárú. Chloisfeá biorán dá dtitfeadh sé. Labhair sí go sona séimh i gcónaí le na daltaí agus mhol sí dóibh féinmheas ceart a bheith acu. Tháinig sí agus d'imigh sí go ciúin, fiú ní chloisfeá an doras á dhúnadh aici agus níor tháinig sí riamh inár dtreo gan cuireadh— bhí sí mar sin. Ní chuirfeadh sí isteach ná amach ar éinne beag ná mór.

Is maith is cuimhin liom tionól urnaithe amháin tráth a raibh páistí Rang a Sé ar tí an scoil a fhágáil ag deireadh na bliana. Bhí na tuistí istigh linn agus chuir sí téip ar siúl dúinn faoi imeacht na bpáisti. Ansin labhair sí linn agus ní dhearmadfá go deo í agus í a' rá nach linn na páistí ar chur ar bith agus go mbeidis páirteach i nglúin nach mbeadh aon teagmháil againn leo. Cinnte bhí an ceart ar fad aici.

Is cuimhin liom freisin nuair a fuair Cathal bás i dtubaiste ar an bhfeirm, bhí sí linn ar scoil ag tacú le gach éinne agus ag guí linn. Nach fíor é gurbh in am an ghátair is ea a thuigtear na cairde. Bhí sí linn freisin nuair a d'éag Paula agus Bríd agus ba mhór an chabhair a treoir agus a paidreacha a bheith linn.

Bhí an-mheas aici ar chúrsaí Gaeilge agus ba mhinic a bhreathnaigh sí ar dhrámaí Gaeilge dúinn chun an grúpa ab fhearr a roghnú. Fiú chaith sí seal amuigh i dtobar na teangan in Inis Oírr agus í ag machnamh di féin ar chúrsaí chreidimh agus ag déanamh a fiche dícheall chun dul níos giorra chun Dé.

Le linn na hochtóidí reachtáil sí grúpaí leanaí chun dul chuici ag guí sna tráthnónaí agus ba mhór an dea-thionchar a bhí aici orthu. Bhí ardmheas ag na páistí i gcónaí uirthi agus thaitin a

cuairteanna ar an scoil go mór leo. Bhí an t-ádh leo casadh léi agus bhí an t-ádh leis an scoil gur sheol Dia inár measc í. D'fhág sí cuimhní cinn a mhairfidh go deo agus threisigh sí an Chríostaíocht i ngach éinne a chuir aithne uirthi.
Go dtuga Dia solas na bhFlaitheas di.

Deaglán Ó Céilleachair
Inis

I give thanks to God for the beautiful blessing which he gave me in my friendship with Sr Eucharia.

When I first met her I was not a Catholic. I was attending mass, sometimes, but unable to receive our Lord Jesus in the Eucharist. The words that remain in my mind from my first meetings with Sr Eucharia are, 'Wouldn't you like to receive Jesus in the Eucharist? You might want to think about becoming a Catholic'.

Three months later, and this was the case. I was receiving our Lord, body, blood, soul and divinity in the Eucharist, God's precious sacrament of love, this beautiful gift of himself, hidden under the mere appearance of bread and wine, really present in the Eucharist, was now God's gift to me. The same Jesus who had been with his first disciples on the road to Emmaus was with me, the only difference being the manner in which he was present.

How can I ever thank Sr Eucharia and all those others who directed me towards this sacramental presence? Sr Eucharia, who was so much in love with our Lord, spoke frequently to me of his great love for us, especially of his eucharistic love.

Today I have the privilege of studying theology in Rome – certainly not because of any merits of my own, but by the grace of God and through the prayers of many people and especially those of dear Eucharia. She continually prayed for me over all the fourteen years that I knew her and I do believe that she will now continue doing so. Like St Therese of Lisieux, who said, 'I want to spend my heaven doing good on earth', I can imagine Sr Eucharia continuing to work for me and for the good of souls. Therefore, as I now remember her, I smile. I smile because of all the love she showed me and because she will continue to be close to me as I move forward in my life with God.

Thank you so much, dear Sr Eucharia!

Praised be Jesus and Mary and all the Holy Angels and Saints!

Denise Oliver
Newcastle upon Tyne, England

My memories of Sr Eucharia are all fond and very close to my heart. When we first moved here from England, it was herself and Sr Geraldine who came to our house with a welcoming gift. A friendly, neighbourly gesture and its memory has remained with us since then.

I had been attending a Catholic church before our move here and I had decided that I would convert to the Catholic faith. Sr Eucharia was my teacher, an extremely wise and knowledgeable woman with the patience to explain all kinds of things. My weekly lessons were enjoyable as she shared her own vast knowledge of the Catholic faith, and frequently it seemed to be no more than just a simple 'chat' in her relaxing company, and one which always finished with some tea and cake.

One day when I had to organise a party, I left with her a 'mystery guest' who was in fact a priest from England and a family friend. Of course she made him very welcome with not only chat, but tea and apple pie as well. Indeed, he felt so much at home that when I came back to collect him he decided to stay longer and to offer mass! He talks about her to this day.

I used to work in the village shop. Sr Eucharia was a customer who would always be in good form. She loved wild birds and used to buy small packets of nuts. She also used to try new foods and recipes; indeed I often knew what she would like and so would save some special things for her. I can remember too that she would always smell of lavender and every time I smell it now, I fondly think of her.

Sr Eucharia touched the hearts of everyone; she was certainly a gift from God.

Carol Andrews
Corofin

Eucharia had a wonderful sense of humour; she loved a good joke and could tell one as well. However, just as naturally as one breathes, she could turn any conversation towards God. She could rise to a mystic level of enthusiasm when referring to the Father's love and to his presence in our daily lives.

Not that Eucharia was all softness. If some criticism was appropriate, she was not slow to give it. For example, she would say, 'What is the point of seeking vocations when the family is falling apart? Good Christian families nurture vocations. We must support the Christian family first'. Eucharia was a practical, no-nonsense woman. She taught me how to bake brown bread and scones and I can still recall her sitting in the autumn sunshine as she stitched a zip on my godchild's skirt for school.

Eucharia's practical life was very full. She loved the people of the village and wanted always to be helping, listening and consoling them. She herself would never speak about the social work she did, but I have heard from others of her visits to the lonely and the sick.

Every morning Eucharia attended mass in Corofin at 10.00 a.m. So did I, whenever possible. We would then go back to her house (or occasionally to mine) for a cuppa and a chat, that is, when she did not have any other business to attend. I, in either case, would frequently unburden my own soul and then Eucharia would lift up all my troubles and my joys to God and set my heart at rest.

One morning when Eucharia was not at mass (she had been earlier, I discovered), I knocked anxiously on her door. The footsteps coming down the stairs reassured me.

'You were at prayer', I said.
'Yes', she answered, with her heart-warming smile.
'May I join you?' I asked.
'Yes.'

And we climbed the stairs together to her little sanctuary for the Blessed Sacrament, where we prayed in silence until it was time for coffee.

Later, when Eucharia left for Ennis, she would walk to the Friary church for mass at 10.00 a.m. (I usually phoned her when I was able to go in.) We would then often drive, with coffee on the way, to Ballyalla Lake, or we would simply walk in the convent garden. There was always a visit to the Blessed Sacrament to conclude.

The best fun we ever had (and there was always laughter with Eucharia) was the impulsive visit which we paid to the Cathedral in Loughrea to see the Evie Hone windows. We never drove too far because of my imperfect sight but I had the idea that Loughrea was no more than a few miles out the road! The journey was at first unsettling and seemed to be going on forever but Eucharia was not perturbed, even when we had to turn on entering Loughrea so as to avoid the town. We simply could not find the Cathedral for hours and then, when we eventually found it, we discovered that there was a drawn-out wedding service being held. 'They are only at the Gospel!' Eucharia exclaimed and later, after half an hour, 'You go in, I'm not well up on Evie Hone'!

Because of my defective sight, I did not get to see Eucharia too often after she had gone to Limerick. I was sorry about that and I missed her terribly.

Dearest Eucharia, it was an honour and privilege to be your friend.

Rose Macnamara
Corofin

The only thing necessary
is our personal relationship with God.
Everything else follows.

Eucharia had a universal outlook; she saw the whole picture. She was a very intelligent woman and was a psychologist to many. She did a lot of good in the community and if she had a key to the kingdom of heaven she would let everybody in. If she had not chosen the path to God, which was through the Mercy congregation, she would certainly have made a wonderful wife and mother but, of course, in her chosen vocation all the people of the world were hers.

She was very good to the poor and charitable to all. She had a great sense of humour and would enjoy the banter that would go on during a conversation. She also had her own sad times and was never afraid to show that side of herself to the world.

Minnie Kenny
Corofin

I knew Sr Eucharia for the best part of twenty-five to thirty years, and there are so many stories I could tell. But the one that stands out in my mind took place in 2004.

I was very troubled at the time as my past had come back to haunt me, and I must say that she was the perfect listener. Listening for me is a three-way prong. You listen with your ears, you listen with your eyes and you listen with your heart. What I mean is that when I was pouring out my heart to Eucharia she could hear the pain in my voice and she could see the pain in my eyes and she could feel the pain in my heart. When I was finished, we hugged and the tears were flowing and I knew that I was being healed. I left renewed and I have not looked back since.

To me, any time I was alone with Sr Eucharia was like as if I was with the Lord. As if the two were one, and I'm certain that they were! Sr Eucharia was a very special person and a friend to me and because no matter where I met her, whether in a group or by herself, I always saw her beautiful little smile and always felt the love and peace that radiated from her.

She let the Lord use her completely and, by God, he did.

Love you always.

Donie Tobin
Shannon Town

Mimi and I have both very pleasant memories of Eucharia. She was so patently good and open – open to every person and open to new ideas and perspectives.

As a patient she had a detachment from her own health, while at all times prepared to follow medical advice – this being rarer than you might think.

Frank Counihan
Ennis

Eucharia (I always think of her without the 'Sister') was for me a presence, not always accessible but always there. Effectively that is what she became for me, from that winter's night so many years ago when she engaged me on the telephone, not knowing me as anything but 'Frank's wife'. She spoke about her own life's path and of how only Jesus could give her the fullness of the love she sought. She spoke with such a quiet urgency and with a strange directness that was startling. I imagine Jesus in his own encounters may have done so too.

Mind you, the shaft of light which comes at such a time can also be enough to dazzle, so the way ahead might not be quite as clear for everyone as it could be for her. But she was patient with this stumbler, and it must be said that she was always ready with a gee-up and a firm little nudge to bring me onto the path.

I remember being desolate when she went off to Inis Oírr. But it was Corofin that offered in the end the balance she required, between her great desire to be alone and her own need to serve the rest of us.

Many of us, the fortunate ones, will remember the course that she gave on prayer. Who could have done it better? (That, when she turned down the lights, I drifted off to sleep is neither here nor there!) Even as one who was just on the edge of Eucharia's outer circle (think how wide a one that was!) I find myself wanting to express much more than I am able.

Mimi Counihan
Ennis

Prayer cannot develop
without silence
and recollection/mindfulness.

I met Eucharia when I came to live in Corofin as a priest, working in the Social Services but being available for duty in the parish on weekends. She too had worked in Clare Care in its early days and it was great to chat with her about it and especially about the people who would come as clients. That was my first inkling of her love for people in their ordinary lives and of her certainty that God loved all of them just as they were. She did not believe in any church or gospel or any social service which tried to make people 'better'; her church and gospel saw us all as Christ himself sees us, that is, with love and mercy and deep understanding. Making people 'better' would for her have been like trying to improve on the Mona Lisa!

It took a while for me to notice that, and then to understand the reason why Eucharia was not a reader, nor a Eucharist minister. But it was my failure to perceive that she really understood the term 'to take a lead' and that the challenge it implied for her was more demanding than that which a role in any liturgy could be. It was that of being there with people as they are and of listening. She was sure that she was in God's presence when another human being came to her, no matter what the moment nor what their story was. She loved the liturgy in our church as much because it was about the people who assembled as it was about their God.

I found she had great skill in telling people something true about themselves without it being just *plámás*. When she said anything like this it was as if the Lord himself had taken note. Moreover, what she saw and heard were not, perhaps, the obvious things. She noted gestures, smiles, movements, the beauty of a morning, the million and one other things that many take for granted and she saw God in them all. Then she told someone else, and that is what evangelising means.

I didn't meet Eucharia as often as I would have liked as our daily patterns did not overlap too much, but I was always conscious of her prayerful presence at the heart of our community. In the words of Peter, 'it was good to have been here' while she was living in our midst.

(Fr) Ger Nash
Corofin

We first met Eucharia in 1987 after we came to Corofin from England to live. After mass one morning, as I left the church, Eucharia approached me with a very warm welcome and invited me to her home for a cup of coffee. It became the first of many visits, both to the small house near the heritage centre and then to 'Emmaus'. Over the years, Glen and myself attended her prayer groups and found great peace and love in her presence. We remember one occasion in particular when we took her for a spin around the coast of Clare from south to north; she was delighted as we drove on roads she had never seen before. We also took her to Glenstal Abbey once where we met and had tea with one of the monks, a friend of hers. Then when Glen and I were celebrating our own golden wedding anniversary we were proud and privileged to have her company at a special mass in the Ennis Friary Oratory.

After she left Corofin and went to Ennis, we continued to visit her and were always met with the same friendliness and love. It soon became apparent to us that leaving Corofin had a profound effect on her. Many times she told us how she missed the place and all the dear friends she had made there over many years and how much she looked forward to returning.

When she finally went to McAuley House our visits became sad but, even when in obvious pain, our most dear friend was always kind and generous. She was the perfect hostess still and we received our usual cup of tea and cake. As time went on, however, we observed her failing health. Alas, we were away in England when she went to her own Maker whom she loved and so we were unable to attend the funeral. A lovely lady and a most dear friend had left us, but we know that she is looking down on us and will continue praying for us, as we will for her.

Rest in Eternal Peace until we meet again.

Lilian and Glen Foy
Corofin

I live by the Gospel.
The basis of the Rule and Constitutions
is the Gospel.

I first met Sr Eucharia in 1987. I was working with Sr Geraldine and had been invited, along with my friend Máire, to meet Eucharia before joining the contemplative prayer group that she led. It was a winter evening. Eucharia cooked us a delicious meal and talked and listened to us and affirmed what we were doing in our lives while serving us and making us feel welcome in her home. She was so homely and natural, so understanding and non-judgemental and so different to what I had expected. The evening ended with a profoundly moving prayer time by the open fire. The four of us were united in prayer and the presence of the Lord was palpable. 'Where two or three of you are gathered in my name, there am I in your midst.' What an introduction! I wanted to experience more of this depth of prayer and I did. I went regularly to the Monday night prayer group for the next six years or so and was enriched by Eucharia's leadership and by the input of the other members. I was blessed to have been part of such a special community.

Eucharia was a gifted spiritual guide, teacher and prayer group leader. Her focus was on building up our self-esteem; she never let the focus fall on herself. She always told us that Christ's message could come equally to us and she constantly reminded us that we were future leaders of community and that Christ was being born in us on a daily basis and, through us, could touch the lives of others in the world. This was certainly true of herself.

Eucharia regularly showed me Christ in situations where I could not find him myself. Her advice always surprised me because she never relied on Church teachings but on her knowledge of Christ's presence and of his unconditional love for all. Her wisdom flowed from her own deep relationship with Jesus and it always moved me to a deeper knowledge of his love and his compassion for me in whatever situation I found myself.

Eucharia was a free spirit. She believed that Christ wanted us to be truly free and she questioned anything that restricted freedom of spirit. Institutions challenged her enormously and she constantly gave examples from nature to teach us that God intended us to be free. She used to enjoy reading from a poem about Christ's love for Mary Magdalene by Pádraig Pearse and was particularly amused by the line, 'Oh woman with the wild thing's heart', which she would repeat knowingly. She believed that Jesus could reach us best in our wild sinful nature and could lure us to himself by love from that strange place. She spoke about the gentleness and vulnerability of God who waits and longs for our friendship. I loved her teaching about religion, which I wrote down and kept in my bible: 'Religion is a free surrender to the Almighty and Transcendent God who enters gently, even hesitantly, into our lives.'

Eucharia's own dream was to withdraw into solitude with her beloved Christ to continue her life of prayer in a hermitage surrounded by nature. She would pray for the world from there and would continue to be available to people who wanted to come to her to talk or to pray. One of the prayers she loved and shared was the following from the Celtic Tradition:

Hermit Prayer
O son of the living God, old eternal King,
I desire a hidden hut in the wilderness that it may be my home.

A narrow little blue stream beside it and a clear pool
for the washing away of sin through the grace of the Holy Ghost.

A lovely wood close about it on every side, to nurse birds
with all sorts of voices and to hide them with its shelter.
Looking south for heat and a stream through its land,
and good fertile soil suitable for all plants.

A beautiful draped church, a home for God from heaven,
and bright lights above the clean white Gospels.

Enough of clothing and food from the King of fair fame,
and to be sitting for a while and praying to God in every place.

There is a special place in the Burren near Eagle's Rock called St Macduagh's Bed. It was the hermitage of St Colman Macduagh who later founded the monastery at Kilmacduagh. When I go there I always think of Eucharia and of her dream and of the hermit's prayer that describes the place so well.

One of my last meetings with Eucharia was in November 2002, soon after her return to the convent in Ennis. I met her on the street on a cold day. She was returning from the church to the convent. I expected her spirit to be sad but, as always, Eucharia surprised me. She was chuckling to herself and with twinkling eyes she said, 'You know, the Lord has a great sense of humour. Not enough is written about his sense of humour. He gets a great kick out of the way we look at things in our lives'. We talked for a few minutes and I went home with a profound sense of Christ's presence and of knowing more of him through Eucharia's deep faith and through her knowledge of him. Again she had blessed me by incarnating Jesus into my life.

Thank you, Eucharia, for your life and your love. Your devotion to your beloved Christ has enriched my spiritual life enormously. Your spirit is alive and still with us.

Emer Ní Mhaoileoin
Ennis

When I think of Sr Eucharia, which is often, a number of images come to mind. Her face, with the trust and openness of a child's and the wisdom of the ages. Her hands and the simple silver band encircling a lifetime of fidelity to the Lord and of dedication to other people. Her gentleness: there was a waif-like energy that surrounded her. Her solidity: she seemed to have no need of earthly things. Her frailty: behind her strength there were wide eyes that looked out on the world and a heart that could be hurt. Her humour: she had a way of laughing that was just short of a chortle, contagious, special. Utterly convinced that God had a great sense of humour, she laughed with the conviction of a person who had spent sufficient time in the presence of her friend to know and to appreciate our quirkiness in his eyes.

I remember my first meeting with Eucharia in Corofin. I had been brought there for the night by Sister Geraldine as a problem in hotel arrangements meant I did not have a room in Limerick beside the University where I was to lecture the next day. Eucharia ran, I'm sure she ran, with arms outstretched to meet me and I felt the way that children feel when they are being welcomed home. There was nowhere else on earth to be but there. There with her. 'Was there no room at the inn?' she asked. 'Then you must have been sent here'.

And so I believe I was, so that I would have the privilege of knowing her and carrying with me, ever after, an appreciation of how uncomplicated, how embracing, how giving life could be. That, in an uncertain world, people like her still lived their lives for others! That there was still the countryside, places like Corofin, people not disconnected from the earth, the seasons, the changing light, the sounds and sights that cannot be heard or seen in the city! To know that there were places of total peace, of acceptance, of hospitality, of humour and of conversation by a fire! To know that she was there!

There are two further images that arise when I think of Eucharia. One is of a sparrow, held gently between two hands: a card she sent me, that for me was symbolic of Eucharia, held, embraced, loved and beauteous in his hands. When her time in Corofin was over, I thought of her as a bird whose chirp was silenced, caged, aching to be free, longing to fly home.

There is another card Eucharia sent me. 'This card was specially chosen for you', she said in a letter that also told me about her preparations to leave Corofin. 'The beginning of the end of my time in Corofin,' she wrote. 'I shall miss the place and especially the people.' On the front of the card were the words:

> *Blessed are you*
> *Woman of wisdom,*
> *Enfolding, unfolding mystery and myth,*
> *Revealing truth and light*
> *For all who yearn to call themselves free.*

Yes, you were all of those words and more, Eucharia, to those who met you, knew you, loved you and now want to keep you in their memories as well as in their hearts.

Rest in Peace, wise and gentle woman.

Marie Murray
Dublin

I only met Sister Eucharia once and consider myself lucky to have met such a special person. She was staying in Glendalough, Co. Wicklow, when I met her. I spent the afternoon there. We talked about life and death and God. Later we went to pray together.

Having spent that afternoon with Sister Eucharia, I left feeling closer to God. She praised God for his love, humour, mercy, acceptance and forgiveness. I felt enriched by her company. God cares for us and helps us through our struggles and sometimes he does so by sending people like Sr Eucharia to let us know just how much he loves us. She was an embodiment of God's love.

Aisling Emma Murray
Dublin

Sr Eucharia, how we miss you, especially our son Ben, who has special needs.

Our holidays in Corofin will never be quite the same without Sr Eucharia to welcome us back. She always had so much time for Ben and made him feel very special.

He would look forward to their chat after mass each day. She was so interested in how his schooling was going. The most important question was to find out if he was still an altar server. It gave her great joy to know that he loved to serve at least twice a week.

Ben is quite sure that Sr Eucharia is looking down on him from heaven so he still has his little chats with her.

Rest in peace, dear Sr Eucharia.

Mr and Mrs B. Hansford, and Ben
Weybridge, Surrey

Ennis Prayer Group: Memories Recalled

(This group began in 1977/1978. There were monthly meetings. Eucharia became part of the group and made it a prayer group. We discovered that she was a bit of a radical, that she had her own particular slant. We loved to see her coming through the door and we are grateful for all that she did for us.)

A collection of comments:

* She gave us a sense of mystery.
* We were reared with a fear of God. She showed us that he is a God of love. She gave us great courage to keep going on bad days.
* I have a friend who was not a Catholic. She said that Eucharia had told her that the first experience children have of the love of God is the love of their parents. A most profound statement! It helped her to appreciate the love of God.
* God lets nothing happen without good coming from it. She made me see my life in another way. Recently, my grandchild was knocked down by a car. I was on the scene. I was able to be God's hands and feet. That was what Eucharia said we all can be; in fact she said that ours are the only hands and feet he has.
* She loved working with married couples. She could look at everybody with wonderment.
* We were privileged to go to her prayer group. When I came to Ennis from Galway I sometimes felt very broken and lost, spiritually as well as psychologically. One night Mattie, my husband, learned that he was going to be made redundant. I shared my anguish with Eucharia and she helped. I also spoke to her about my children. Eucharia said, 'Margaret, don't be

worrying about your children and the fact that they are moving out. From a practical point of view most young people get a haversack and a backpack and they travel all around the world. Your children are well trained'. This is so: Fr Barry is in Rome, Louise is in Europe, Priscilla is in Knock. I thank God for the wonderful wisdom Eucharia gave to us as a family.

- I have lovely memories of her house in Corofin, the ambience, the simple creative way she did things. There was no fuss. Such a comfortable presence!

- She never saw people as superiors or inferiors – we were all the same.

- Memories mean people never die. She loved farmers. She would go up the village and chat with them. She talked of creation. Even the dogs followed her down to her house! She loved children and had a special prayer group for them. Total dedication to the Lord!

- My first meeting with her was in 1984. Inside the door there was a fire, and the kettle was put on the boiler. I was between finishing teaching and retiring. I had been reading about saints. 'Keep far away from those saints. Most of them are daft. It's all about love.' She exuded joy, patience, kindness, goodness. I brought that away with me. Eucharia helped me to live out of a place in myself.

- The first time I met Eucharia was in Coláiste where she tried to teach me how to cook. Made a better job when she taught me religion! I had a very rigid view of life. Small things worried me, like eating one minute before communion! She said, 'Do you think God has a watch in his hand?' I always waited to see what she would say at sharing in a prayer group. She always had a teaching in it. Eithne (a friend) said, 'I'd love to know Jesus like Eucharia does'. When my husband died Eucharia comforted me with the words, 'he has never left you'.

- She had the gift of wisdom. She could cut through rubbish.
- One day I was bringing her to the Friary. She put lavender on her hand in order to welcome the Lord in communion.
- Ennis was so different from Corofin. The doors were locked; the alarm was on; she was often afraid of coming back late. Her real home was in Corofin.
- Eucharia went through her desolation when she left Corofin. Corofin needs a person like Eucharia. She was a Martha of the gospel. Maura and Donal treated her like a mother.
- Eucharia walked into my life. She came to Glenstal (with Geraldine). I went to Corofin, to the house with the blue door. It was archetypical: man runs after a woman and then gets caught! She's one of the most fascinating people I have ever met. I might find her crossing the bridge and I used to call her a cross between Julian of Norwich and Peg Sayers. I visited her in Ennis hospital when she was sick. I called her 'unencloseable'. She loved that. Eucharia animated Corofin but frequently she would be worried by the thought she was doing something for which she had not been trained. Yet, what she gave was the overflow of her own spiritual goodness. Those around reaped the benefit. She was wonderful – but so were the people who brought out of her that which was waiting to be born.
- She was an inspiration. Our daughter had a health problem and I explained it to Eucharia. She prayed, then every time we met her she asked, 'How is she?' I have no doubt that she helped her and got her back to health. My daughter once said, 'I didn't know her, Mom. Someone had to be praying for me. I felt this nun had a special thing going for me'.

Catherine McAuley
was a woman of action
because she was primarily a woman of prayer.

In Memory of Her

Whatever contact I have with hope is clear to me on certain mornings when a voice slips into my mind like a shy suggestion of love that nothing will deny. It is a passionate and gentle voice, authentic as a patch of sunlight on a floor inside a window.

The above is from Brendan Kennelly's 'A Passionate and Gentle Voice'. For me, Eucharia epitomised these poetic words. In fact, she constantly brought hope to the hopeless in her own charming and disarming way.

'Ah Clare, 'tis great to see you' was Eucharia's constant 'Hello' to me – a greeting so sincere that it made my heart smile. I was privileged and humbled to have been counted among her friends and memories crowd in as I try to pen a simple appreciation in memory of her. Eucharia's striking characteristic for me was that she was always for, prophetically for, so much. She didn't waste time being against. Didn't she walk out of chapter disappointed, or was it disgusted, that we were wasting time talking about the length of our habits. 'I'm going down to the thrift shop to talk to the poor.' We tried to make her stay; she left and we were the poorer!

Eucharia was for the poor – no bugle, just a heart of love.

She was also for:

- Contemplative prayer.
- A way of life that nourished goodness, gifts and courage.
- Women, as a matter of justice and a ministry of mercy.
- Nurturing questions and a kind of holy indifference to the set pieces that might be offered as answers. Questions themselves were sacramental for her.
- Small Christian communities of lay people.
- Small Mercy communities; she had a great sense of unease with the centrality of distant authority figures in the amalgamated setting. Amalgamation never rested easily with Eucharia.

Eucharia's contemplative prayer life kept her at peace with her prophetic role among her Mercy listeners and her lay communities. There was room in her Everest heart for us all and the seat by the fire was always there: the fire of her love for God, the fire of her enthusiasm for the gospel, the fire of a disciple's tongue urging you to walk in their footsteps, no matter how hard or painful it might be. Somehow, like Walter Bruggeman, she knew that 'hope is only born when pain is articulated', and so she listened to each story until it turned into hope for the storyteller. I know this is true; it happened to me on many of my 'steps' on the road. She could read my heart and I am so grateful for that. Always she had the immortal one-liners, for example 'You deal with lies by living your truth'.

At one particularly dark time, when my thoughts were out of control, creating a level of confusion, she wrote me a card. The photo on the front was powerful; the cryptic message of inspiration, affirmation and hope was all I needed. It said, 'May your Christmas be a truly happy one. I know you will continue to be a light to his people as you ever have been. The Lord is with you; his people need you. What else matters? Love, Eucharia'.

Grace came to me yet again from God's messenger of peace, love and hope. Somehow, I believe that Eucharia's passionate and gentle voice, ever prophetic, will continue to challenge and inspire us.

Eucharia, old friend, I wish there were two of you – but maybe there are because I glimpse you in the innocence and guilessness of my grandniece, in the moments of graced courage that spring into my lips unexpectedly and in the heart when I manage to utter the truth in ways that you inspired. You live on, old friend – you live on. You were wonderful; pray for us that we may wonder like you did, in the heart and in the soul. You, who are calmly resting in God, but so alert to all who are around you.

Sr Clare Slattery, RSM
Nenagh

Sr Eucharia was a Sister of Mercy whose compassion was boundless and whose community embraced everyone who crossed their path. People from all walks of life were drawn to her and she was equally at home talking to the Lord in the church, chatting with a friend on the street or visiting families in their homes.

I was privileged to have known Eucharia during two periods of challenging change in her life. My earliest memories of her date from when she answered the Lord's call and started working full-time among the poor of Ennis. The choice of this 'less-trodden road' was not wholly understood by many of her sisters in community and she sometimes was a thorn in the side of local government officials too.

Her philosophy of life, so much in evidence in her preferential option for the poor, was inspirational. Her love of Jesus in the

Eucharist was the source of her wisdom and of the spiritual teaching that she shared with the Charismatic Prayer Group in the Friary Hall. All her conversations were about making the Kingdom of God real for everyone.

I was her chauffeur sometimes when she needed to travel out of town on her myriad works of mercy, though she did learn to drive her blue Mini OZ1. She was concerned about traveller families on the roadside and other families on the margins of society and she gladdened many hearts with her gifts of clothing and of food. In the late 1960s, while she was still teaching, Eucharia became involved with raising awareness of the plight of travelling people and she championed their cause, even going to court to plead on their behalf. Her practical projects included a thrift shop on O'Connell Street in Limerick and a quilt-making afternoon in Our Lady's School – recycling initiatives benefiting both the giver and receiver. Her warm personality as well as her deeply spiritual talks encouraged others to volunteer in the projects she initiated. She saw the need for trained social workers in the development of the social services and was delighted when the Little Sisters of the Assumption came to Ennis.

Clare Social Services, Clare Care today, was well established when Eucharia went to live in Corofin in 1981. She continued her ministry of prayer and nurtured prayer groups in 'Emmaus' and in people's homes in Corofin, on Inis Oírr and elsewhere in the county. Her belief in the Apostolate of the Laity bore fruit in young and old and she was loved by all.

Sadly, her radiance dimmed in the convent to which she returned after living for twenty-two years in Corofin. Used to solitude in 'Emmaus' she was burdened by the necessity of living with a large number of Sisters here in St Xavier's. Again I was fortunate to spend time with her and to be refreshed by her wisdom and her love of God. But the Lord had a further cross for her to bear. Eucharia went to hospital in May and during her long, lingering illness, which she suffered patiently, she knew little of the joy that she had shared so generously in all her ministries. In her lonely struggle, her beloved Jesus had hidden his face from her. The nurses and all who cared for her in McAuley House were conscious of her serenity, her gratitude and her prayerfulness.

Eucharia died peacefully on Holy Thursday night, the feast of the Eucharist. It was a blessing to be with her as she gently went to meet her God. Eucharia was special. 'The good she did lives after her.' She will always live in our hearts.

Sr Anne O'Grady, RSM
Ennis

The individual can have true wisdom if he is capable of listening.
Plato

Eucharia was capable of listening and she had true wisdom.

She was special because she drew people to her. She drew people because she listened and because of her depth of soul. In periods of cultural upheaval and disorientation she stood apart. At a time when there was, and still is, an ongoing search for direction and meaning she was a quiet presence – one to whom others could turn.

The phrase 'it was the best of times, it was the worst of times', from Dickens's *A Tale of Two Cities*, is often used these days. These are the best of times in that we are the best fed, best clothed, best housed, best schooled generation ever to have lived in Ireland. However, growing numbers are wondering, 'Where are we going?' Often it appears that we are left without a compass while on a journey. And in that sense these times are not good.

In the eyes of a great number of people, the Institution of the Church has failed to provide them with the kinds of support and resources necessary for authentic spiritual transformation. But down through history when the Institution seemed incapable of responding to the human and spiritual needs of people, a prophet emerges to show the way for others to follow. Eucharia was that prophet for our times and an undernourished people were attracted to her as she listened and responded to their human needs. She was the one who showed that 'spirituality' is not something about spirits or other-worldly phenomena. It is about discovering one's self, about being at peace with oneself and becoming more in touch with a deeper sense of purpose.

Eucharia's was a practical spirituality that had its origins in the human condition. She realised that many, if not all, of our problems originated from inner, human issues. Behind every problem were human decisions, human thinking, human values and human self-centredness. And we tend to look for solutions in the world around us, rather than within ourselves, where the problem originated. She led people to the root problem rather than just dealing with the symptoms. I always felt she had a very simple but practical approach to spiritual well-being. Her quiet presence, her emphasis on 'being', her own inner freedom and security conveyed something very powerful to those who came in contact with her. Her presence and her house became a haven for people living through a period of technological revolution and coming out of a century when institutions shaped our lives and wrote the script for us, a time of extraordinary material developments. She pointed the way and clearly indicated that this present century would be about the spiritual or nothing. Are we not already reaching saturation in a consumer culture? Events are bringing this home to us. She was indeed a woman for our time.

Eucharia was before her time in indicating that the most important question we need to be asking is, 'How can we free the mind to allow it to be more at peace and more compassionate?' She also clearly indicated that the old ways are not working, that the Church has to become more Christ-centred and his message and values need to be connected with our lives.

Eucharia was a beacon guiding many of us through the human story to a wonder and an awe and to a deep sense of the sacred and the mystical, thus rediscovering ourselves.

(Fr) Harry Bohan
Shannon Town

His love endures forever.

Celebration of the Life of Sr Eucharia Keane

Sister of Mercy & Parishioner of Corofin, Kilnaboy & Rath

5.00 p.m. Saturday, 26 March 2005

MC (Leonard Cleary): Welcome to this Church service to celebrate the life of Eucharia. In accordance with Eucharia's view of the importance of the laity, religious and clergy working together in the Church, this service will be led by and will involve all partners in the parish. Thus, we begin our service as Eucharia is formally received and welcomed home by Frank and Maura representing all her neighbours and friends and by Fr Ger, our resident priest. During these prayers Sean will sprinkle Eucharia's coffin with holy water.

Procession

Event	Location	Leader
Arrival of remains	Bridge Street	Undertaker
Roads closed by Gardaí; Stewards on Main Street, Church Street and Bridge St; Heritage Centre Car Park available for Sisters of Mercy		Willie Corbett Donal Cleary

Guard of Honour		Paddy McMahon Sean O'Brien
Brief words, outside 'Emmaus', setting the tone for the service		Maura Clancy
Funeral procession will be led by three people: a neighbour, a representative of a local family and close friend, and by the resident priest	Bridge Street	Frank Fitzpatrick Maura Cleary Fr Ger Nash
Coffin carried by two teams from house to corner	Bridge Street Church Street	Willie Lahiffe Jimmy Lahiffe Tony Neylon Val Egan
and from corner to church		Gussy O'Loughlin John Cahill Ollie O'Loughlin Christy O'Loughlin

Church Service

Choir, playing and singing		Choir
The remains will then be formally received and welcomed by the three people who lead the procession		Frank Fitzpatrick Maura Cleary Fr Ger Nash

Address to the person of
Eucharia
Sprinkling of coffin   Sean O'Brien
with holy water

Scripture Pieces

Reading of the   Tony Neylon
'Institution of the Eucharist'   Fr Ger Nash
and the significance of Eucharia's
death on Holy Thursday

Eucharistic theme   Choir

Incense/scented candles   Mary O'Brien

Gifts

Received at top of aisle
– Painting (Sean McDermott)   Willie Corbett
– Cooking/baking   Mary McMahon
– Figurine of Christ   Mena Lahiffe
– Potted plant   Christine Spellman
– Prayer card   Kathleen Corbett
– Bible   Sean McDermott

Emmaus Gospel

Quiet reflection

Prayers of the Faithful

Edel Lahiffe:
   We pray for Eucharia, our sister in Christ,
   who was nourished at the table of our Saviour.
   Welcome her into the halls of the heavenly banquet.
   Lord hear us.

Gary Tierney:

We pray for all who are assembled here
for the homecoming of our friend, Eucharia,
that we may all be gathered together again in God's kingdom.
Lord hear us.

Grainne O'Brien:

We pray for all our deceased relatives and friends.
May Eucharia and all who have helped us
have the reward of their goodness.
Lord hear us.

Maeve Davouren:

We pray for the Sisters of Mercy
who have lost a special sister.
May God bless them in their work.
Lord hear us.

Brief Introduction to readings	Donal Cleary
Matt 19:13-15 *(Let the little children come)*	Pauline Collins
Brief reflection	Fr Maurice Harmon
Suffer Little Children	Choir
A friend's reflection on what	
Corofin meant to Eucharia	Sr Geraldine Collins
Reflective music	Choir
The Lord's Prayer	
Concluding Prayer to Service	Maura Cleary
	Frank Fitzpatrick
	Fr Ger Nash
Coffin into sacristy	Stewards

Choir

Coffin re-emerges and Eucharia rests in repose
People file past coffin in their own time
Overnight vigil

Tribute by Sr Geraldine Collins
(Given during the mass on Easter Monday in Ennis Cathedral)

In the evening of Life we shall be judged by Love.
St John of the Cross

A card in Eucharia's office book contains the following words:

I, Sr Eucharia, take thee, my dear Jesus, to be my heavenly spouse, to have and to hold, from this day forward, for better, for worse, for richer or poorer, in sickness and in health till death do us unite.

On the card is a picture of a young woman (novice) gazing on her spouse, Jesus, who is handing her a crown of thorns.

Eucharia's life, it could be said, is summarised in these two movements – prayer and service. She kept her eyes fixed on the Lord in prayer, love and contemplation, and accepted into herself the pain of the poor and the marginalised, to which she responded with practical service, love and compassion. Her core vision was that everything flows from our relationship with God and our knowledge of his unconditional love for us. 'His faithful love endures forever.'

A poem which she loved expresses her desire to absorb and be consumed by God's love:

> *Let me be still for one more winter.*
> *Let me nestle at my love's feet.*
> *The wild geese fly and my heart cries peace.*
> *Let me rest with my love*
> *Through the long dark nights.*
> *Let me rest, listen to his whisperings,*
> *When spring comes, I will fulfil them.*

She fulfilled them through her practical service of the poor and of all people. She had been called 'the unenclosable Julian' who 'did not make of God a pillow nor of prayer an eiderdown' (Helder Camara). She could not envision prayer without social action, real and costly. Another poem she loved expresses this:

> *When Jesus came to Golgotha, they hanged him on a tree.*
> *They drove great nails through hands and feet and made a Calvary.*
> *They crowned him with a crown of thorns.*
> *Red were his wounds and deep.*
> *For those were crude and cruel days, and human flesh was cheap.*
> *When Jesus came to Birmingham*
> *They simply passed him by.*
> *They never hurt a hair of him,*
> *They only let him die,*
> *For men had grown more tender and they would not give him pain.*
> *They only just passed down the street and left him in the rain.*
> *Still Jesus cried, 'Forgive them, Lord, they know not what they do'.*
> *And still it rained a wintry rain*
> *That drenched him through and through.*

The crowds went home and left the streets
Without a soul to see,
And Jesus crouched against the wall and cried for Calvary.

Eucharia's vision of our responsibility for our sisters and brothers often caused unease and upset. 'Will you tell me is she a great disturber?' someone asked. And Eucharia would repeat it with a twinkle in her eye, 'Is she a great disturber?' At many levels she was, as her life called us out of our ease and comfort zones to what we could become.

In her younger years she was a memorable teacher who left an indelible impression on her pupils in whom she awakened a quest for God. She was later to become 'the travellers' nun', the social worker, the activist, the carer. And every few years she withdrew to spend some months in prayer with her Beloved.

Today, as we reflect on her later years in her beloved Corofin, we think of the open door, the cup of tea by the fire, the listening heart, no judgement, only listening with the heart, totally accepting and understanding. We think of her love for the children who called to the house, one of whom expressed what they felt when she said – 'she's not Eucharia, she's My-caria'!

We think of the fun, the joke on the street, enjoying the people so much, being just what she wanted to be – a good neighbour – giving and receiving love from the people. And always prayer, prayer and prayer groups, where she created a space for people to listen, learn, love, share and know by experience the risen Lord in their midst.

Eucharia was a Mercy Sister. She never took the structures of religious life too seriously, but she lived from the heart of Mercy. She was one of Catherine McAuley's 'walking nuns', radiating love, compassion and humanity, living the essence of gospel / Christian / religious life.

She could be at times impatient with both church and religious life and indeed with any institution which, in her words, 'tried to freeze the paradoxes of the Gospel into frozen formulae'.

At a personal level, her final message to me during her last days will always remain in my heart. At her bedside I would slowly read some of her favourite psalms. She would silently move her lips during the familiar lines, or sometimes sink into a deep silence and stillness. One day, as I read psalm 118 with the refrain 'His faithful love lasts forever', hoping it might comfort her in her pain and distress, she asked me to repeat the phrase again and again. Then she said, 'Do you believe this? Do you know this?' and, like a teacher, she tried to help me to know and realise more deeply that 'his faithful love lasts forever'. It was her final message.

And so today she returns to her Lord, as a bride prepared to meet her husband. Today, she says to us in the words of the Song of Songs:

I hear my Beloved,
see how he comes leaping over the mountains,
bounding over the hills.
See where he stands behind a wall.
My Beloved lifts up his voice and he says to me,
'Come then my love, my lovely one come.
For see: winter is past, the rains are over and gone.
The flowers appear on the earth.
The seasons of glad songs has come.
Come my Beloved,
I shall give you the gift of my love,
the rarest fruits,
the new as well as the old.
I have stored them for you, my beloved'.

Today, Eucharia, as we bid farewell to your earthly existence, we know your ever-present spirit will continue teaching us what you knew well: *His faithful love lasts forever.*

In the evening of life
we will be judged on love.

Souvenirs from her Bedside

(The following were collected by Eucharia
and, if not composed by her,
she made them her own.)

Be present,
O Most Merciful Lord,
and protect us through the silent hours of the night,
so that we
who are wearied
by the changes and chances of this fleeting world
may rest in your eternal changlessness,
through Christ, our Lord.
Amen.

As the watchman looks for the morning,
even so do our eyes wait for you, O Christ.
Come with the dawning of the day
and make yourself known to us
in the breaking of the bread,
for you are our Risen Lord,
for even and ever.
Amen.

May my soul be in such peace,
O my God,
that you may find in it a place
where your silence loves to dwell.
Draw me into that eternal mystery
from whence I come.

We shall always be restless
until we become
that which we have always been,
in God.

'Mane nobiscum, Domine, quoniam advesperascit'
(Stay with us, O Lord, for evening falls – Lk 24:22-29)

Assimilate, utilise the shadows of later life:
enfeeblement, loneliness,
the sense that no further horizon lies ahead.

Discover in Christ-omega
how to remain young, enthusiastic,
full of enterprise.

Beware of thinking that every form of melancholy,
indifference, disenchantment,
is to be identified with wisdom.

Make a place, an uplifting place,
for the end which now draws near
and for the decline of one's powers
to whatever degree God may wish.
'To be ready' has never seemed to mean anything to me
but this: to be straining forwards.

May Christ-omega keep me always young
(and what better argument for Christianity could there be
than an enduring youthfulness
drawn from Christ-omega).

Old age comes from him,
Old age leads to him,
Old age will touch me only in so far
as he wills.

'To be young' means
to be hopeful, energetic, smiling
and clear-sighted.

Accept death in whatever guise it may come
in Christ-omega,
that is within the process of the development of life.

A smile, inward and outward,
means facing with sweetness and gentleness
whatever befalls.

Jesus-omega,
grant me
to serve you,
to proclaim you,
to glorify you,

to make you manifest to the very end.

Desperately, Lord Jesus, I commit to your care
my last active years and my death.
Grant me the grace to end well
in the way
that will best advance
the glory of Christ-omega.
This is the grace of graces.

I go forward to meet the one who comes.

Pentecost

I was there when Peter barred the door.
I watched the others silent in the gloom,
Each pair of eyes so sad and far away,
Each saddened heart remembering the tomb.
Then Andrew said, 'Remember on the lake,
Remember how he called my brother out';
And Peter said, 'My heart was light and gay
And halfway there it sank with fear and doubt'.
Another said, 'I saw him shedding tears,
I heard him stand before the tomb and shout.
I felt the ground beneath me move and sway
As Lazarus all bound in cloth came out'.
And now the voices rang around the room
As others told a tale from days gone by
Of lepers healed, the mad man soothed and stilled,
Of children loved, a Roman soldier's hope,
A cripple filled with joy at newfound feet.

And with their hearts brim-full of joy and peace,
They ran and brought that message to the street.
I was there when hearts were closed and sad,
When hearts were opened, gladdened and set free.
I sat in silence in the Upper Room,
Yes, I was there that day, and so was he.

Most Holy Lord,
the ground of our beseeching,
who, through your servant, Julian,
revealed the wonder of your love.
Grant that, as we are created in your nature
and restored by your grace,
our wills may be so one with yours
that we may come to see you
face to face and gaze on you for ever.
Amen.

Meeting Jesus in the Gospels
(Guidelines used by Sr Eucharia)

Be There with him and for him.
Yes, be there. Have you ever talked with someone who was with you
bodily, but not present to you with attention and heart?

Want Him
Hunger for him. Prepare for his coming and his word as you
would want and eagerly prepare for a visit from the dearest person

in your life. Invite him to reveal and to communicate himself to you, to speak to you and to teach you how to listen deeply to him.

Listen To Him
Listen with faith, deeply and reverently; listen with trust; listen with hunger to be fed by his word; listen with gratitude and in peace, without searching for hidden meanings. Be simple, like a child nestled in its father's lap; peacefully listening to his story.

Let Him
Let him what? Just let him be with you. Let him be for you what he wants to be. Let him love you. Let him speak to you. Let him hold you and console you and forgive you and strengthen you. Let him take you through dryness and darkness, if he prefers. But let him. Trust yourself to him.

Respond To Him in any way you want to or feel moved to. Be genuinely yourself and respond honestly, freely, spontaneously, reverently. Speak what is in your heart; say what you feel, even when you feel like complaining. Remember that when you don't know what to say, the Holy Spirit prays in you. Just speaking or whispering the name of Jesus rhythmically with your breathing, or repeating words of praise and thanks are profoundly prayerful responses.

(Contemplative prayer is more 'listening to' and 'being aware of' God than saying or doing anything. It is more what God does for us than anything we do for him.)

Appendix

Sr Eucharia Keane, St Xavier's, Convent of Mercy, Ennis. R.I.P.

Eucharia was born in Bournea, Templemore on 11 December 1915. She was educated by the Ursuline Sisters in Thurles. She entered St Xavier's, Ennis on 2 February 1936 and was professed on 15 October 1938.

For thirty years, Eucharia taught Home Economics and Religion in Spanish Point and in Coláiste Muire, Ennis. Her practical and creative abilities enhanced her teaching of Home Economics, while her unique capacity for imparting the gospel message and drawing people to Christ is still remembered and cherished by former students.

Eucharia's strong commitment to people on the margins motivated her to become involved in social work. She played a key role in developing services for the marginalised in Ennis and throughout Co. Clare and was involved in founding the present 'Clare Care' and its many social services. She also spent time working among the poor in Dublin, Limerick, London and Leeds.

Her strong attraction to the contemplative life led her to withdraw at various intervals to spend months in prayer. She became deeply involved in prayer ministry. Her magnetic personality and contemplative spirit drew people to prayer and to a desire for a deeper relationship with God. She guided many and started numerous prayer groups all over the county and on Inis Oírr.

In 1981 she moved to Corofin and wanted simply to be 'a good neighbour'. She loved Corofin and its people and was loved deeply in return. Her free spirit found its deepest expression among them.

In her life Eucharia was indeed one of Catherine's 'walking nuns', combining action with contemplation. She had a truly gospel and mercy spirit of compassion and joy.

Ar dheis De go raibh a h-anam dílis.

We offer our sympathy to her sister, Sr Teresa, Presentation Convent, Turner's Cross, Cork, her cousins Donal and Nancy, her Community and friends.

Funeral Arrangements
Farewell Ritual in Catherine McAuley House, Limerick at 2.30 p.m. on Saturday, 26 March. Arrival in St Bridget's Church, Corofin on Saturday at 5.00 p.m. Reposing in St Xavier's Convent, Ennis from 4.00 p.m. on Sunday. Funeral Mass on Monday at 12.00 noon in Ss. Peter and Paul's Cathedral, Ennis. Burial in Drumcliffe Cemetery after mass.

(Mercy fax sent to all the houses in the South-Central Province)

Let me be still for one more winter,
let me nestle at my love's feet.
The wild geese fly
and my heart cries peace.
Let me rest with my love
through the long dark nights.
Let me rest, listen to his whisperings.
When spring comes
I will fulfil them.

And so this springtime, on Easter Monday, we handed Sr Eucharia Keane back to God, after almost ninety years of life.

A native of the Parish of Bournea (near Roscrea), Eucharia entered St Xavier's Convent, Ennis, in 1936 and was professed in October, 1938.

For thirty years she taught in Spanish Point and in Coláiste Muire, Ennis. She is remembered as a teacher who left an indelible impression on her pupils, in whom she awakened a thirst for God. She was one of Catherine McAuley's 'walking nuns', radiating love, compassion and humility, living the essence of the gospel and religious life.

She was later to become the 'travellers' nun', the social worker, the activist and the carer. She played a key role in developing services for the marginalised in Ennis and throughout Co. Clare and was one of the founders of the present Clare Care.

In 1981, Eucharia moved to Corofin, where she established deep ties and connections with its people. She became involved in various prayer groups and guided many on their journey to God. She had a gift for creating a space for people to listen, learn, love and share.

We pray eternal rest on her gentle soul and may all the seeds of faith, hope and love which she planted in her life continue to bear much fruit.

We offer our sympathy to the Mercy community of St Xavier's and to her sister, St Teresa, Presentation Convent, Cork City.

I measc na naomh go raibh sí.

(Parish Newsletter)

Sr Euchaia Keane, St Xavier's, Convent of Mercy, Ennis and late of Main Street, Corofin, died in the loving care of the staff of Catherine McAuley House, Limerick.

Deeply regretted by her loving sister Sr Teresa, Presentation Convent, Cork and by her Community, relatives and many friends. Removal took place on Saturday from Catherine McAuley House, Old Dominick Street to St Brigid's Church, Corofin.

Reposing took place at St Xavier's Convent, Ennis on Sunday. Removal took place to Ennis Cathedral for concelebrated mass on Monday. Chief Celebrant was Bishop Willie Walsh. Also in attendance were Fr Tom Hogan Adm., Fr Jerry Carey Adm., Canon Pat Taffe, Canon Paddy O'Brien, Canon Brendan O'Donghue, Canon Ruben Butler, Fr John Molloy, Fr Paddy Conway, Fr Jerry Kenny, Fr Michael McNamara, Fr Brian Geoghehan, Fr Ambrose Tinsley, OSB, Fr Michael McLoughlin, Fr Michael Collins, Fr Bernard Canning (diocese of Paisley), Fr Michael McInerney, Fr Joe McMahon, Fr Peadar O'Loughlin, Fr Joseph Condron, OFM (Friary Guardian), Fr Diarmuid O'Riain OFM, Fr Tim Touhy, Fr John O'Brien, Fr Kevin Hogan.

In her earlier days, she was on the teaching staff at Coláiste Muire. Two of her late brothers were priests of the diocese. She was a founder-member of Clare Social Services. For over thirty years she was in residence at Corofin.

(Clare Champion, *Friday, 1 April 2005*)

A dedicated Irish nun who was a champion of the marginalised has died, aged eighty-nine.

Sr Eucharia Keane, who died in Ennis, Co. Clare, devoted herself to this mission following thirty years of teaching in local

Sisters of Mercy schools, earning her the title 'travellers' nun' for her work with gypsies [sic].

Sr Keane was a founder of Clare Care, an agency which works for the needy of all ages and conditions.

(The Universe, *Sunday, 24 April 2005*)

List of Contributors

Sr Teresa Meaney
Sr Frances Xavier Corry
Sr Paul Byrne
Sr Benedict Kenny, RSM
Kathleen Ryder
Mary Macnamara
Fionnuala Moran (Hensey)
Mary Healy
Marie Burke (née Kennedy)
Fr Brian Geoghegan
Nell Foster-Smith
Sr Philomena O'Daly, LSA
Sr Claude McDonald, LSA
Pat Galvin
Michael McDonagh
Mrs McCarthy
Mrs McDonagh
Pam Stotter
Sr Geraldine Fitzgerald, LCM
Bridie Cooling
Carmel Diamond
Mike and Fran Watt
Sr Canice Hanrahan, RSM

Ada Power
Maura Cleary
Donal Cleary
Mary Ellen Nagle
Sean and Mary McDermott
Christina Linnane
Máire Kennedy
A Priest
Christine Kearney
Bernadette Byrne
Edel Lahiffe
Anne Byrne
A Friend
Lena Macnamara
Frank Fitzpatrick
Bridie Malone
Willie and Kathleen Corbett
Mena Lahiffe
Willie, Eileen and Stephen Lahiffe
Geraldine Carrigg
John and Kathleen O'Loughlin
Gus O'Loughlin
Marguerite and Mervyn Groves
Doreen Walker
Mary O'Brien
Leonard Cleary
Deaglán Ó Céilleachair
Denise Oliver
Carol Andrews
Rose Macnamara
Minnie Kenny
Donie Tobin
Frank Counihan
Mimi Counihan

Fr Ger Nash
Lilian and Glen Foy
Emer Ní Mhaoileoin
Marie Murray
Aisling Emma Murray
Mr and Mrs. B. Hansford and Ben
The Ennis Prayer Group
Sr Clare Slattery, RSM
Sr Anne O'Grady, RSM
Fr Harry Bohan